PARALYMPICS

Authors, Dr. R.D. Steadward & Cynthia Peterson

D0617495

ONE SHOT HOLDINGS PUBLISHING DIVISION

Copyright © 1997 Dr. Robert Steadward, Cynthia Peterson & Robert Peterson

All rights reserved. No part of this book may be reproduced or transmitted in any form or by any means, electronic or mechanical, including photocopying, scanning and recording, or by any information storage or retrieval system without prior written permission of both the copyright owner and the authors, except for brief passages quoted in a review.

CANADIAN CATALOGUING IN PUBLICATION DATA

Steadward, R. D.
    Paralympics

    Includes index.
    ISBN 0-9682092-0-3
    1. Paralympics. I. Peterson, Cynthia J. (Cynthia Jane), 1950- II. Title.
    GV709.3.S73 1997   796'.0456
    C97-910526-9

Distributed by:
Alberta Northern Lights Wheelchair Basketball Society
6792-99 Street
Edmonton, Alberta, Canada T6E 5B8
Phone (403) 433-4310
Fax (403) 431-1764
Email: anlwbs@planet.eon.net

Digital Art Work, Cover and Page Design: JDI Design
Production by Bob Peterson

General Notice:
Product names used in this book are for identification purposes only and may not be registered trademarks, trademarks or trade names of their respective owners. The authors disclaim any and all rights in those marks.

Printed and bound in Canada
by DW Friesens Ltd.

TABLE OF CONTENTS

PREFACE

"I can do so much more than I thought I could. The secret is to try."
(Gary McPherson)

The people profiled here are successful not only in the world of disablity sport, but in mainstream society as well. The strong message that comes through so many times is that people with disabilities can overcome the barriers they face. Dr. Robert Steadward, President of the International Paralympic Committee, says of the athletes he coached, "They never thought that their disabilities would in any way limit their ambition, or their ability to participate in anything they wanted to do."

The story of the Paralympic Games is the story of volunteers, thousands and thousands of volunteers, who over the years have made tremendous sacrifices to improve the lives of those with disabilities. It is the story of skilled professionals whose research and commitment benefits not only athletes, but all people with disabilities. It is the story of elite athletes, and the system that supports their success. Here we tell the stories of people who are role models for those in every walk of life.

We want to inspire you. Whether you have found yourself suddenly disabled, or you're looking for reassurance that your efforts can make a difference in the life of a loved one with a disability, or you're a discouraged volunteer who needs to see that you can make a difference, or whether you're a lover of sports looking for insight into the success strategies of elite athletes, the people of the Paralympic movement will help you see your own potential with new clarity.

As one of the slogans developed by Joey Reiman (Brighthouse Ad Agency) for the Atlanta Games says,

"The Olympics is where heroes are made. The Paralympics is where heroes come."

FOREWARD

By the President
of the International Olympic Committee
Juan Antonio Samaranch
Marqués de Samaranch

On behalf of the Olympic movement, I would like to welcome the publication of *Paralympics: Where Heroes Come*, a work by Dr. Robert Steadward, President of the International Paralympic Committee (IPC), and Ms. Cynthia Peterson. Dr. Steadward is the first president of the IPC, an organization that has, under his guidance, become a force for unity among the many categories of adapted sport. IPC's membership has grown from 37 national committees to 150 in less than ten years, making the Paralympic Games an increasingly universal event for disabled athletes all over the world. Indeed, following the Games of the XXVI Olympiad, the Centennial Games, in Atlanta, the X Paralympic Games were host to more than 3,500 athletes from 120 countries, including 44 developing countries.

Dr. Steadward is uniquely qualified to write the history of Paralympic competition, for he has been involved in every level of its organization. As a young volunteer coach for wheelchair athletes, he began the career that has made such a profound contribution to the development of disabled sport. Aware of the importance of education and training for all athletes, both during their years of competition and in the transition to post-competition life, Dr. Steadward has also been seminal in establishing facilities for research and instruction in the fields of sport and physical activity for the disabled.

The precept that all sports should be open to all athletes is one of the guiding principles of the Olympic Movement, and the organization of the Paralympic Games therefore constitutes an important contribution to the universality of the Olympic Movement. I am certain that the entire Olympic family joins me in encouraging the IPC to pursue its groundbreaking work in unifying and consolidating the sports movement for the disabled, about which this new book has much to teach us all.

MESSAGE FROM THE MINISTER

ALBERTA

COMMUNITY DEVELOPMENT

Office of the Minister

Paralympics–Where Heroes Come is a story of courage and success. It is a story of people who overcame barriers to make a difference in their communities–in sport, education, politics, science and the arts.

It is a story of dedicated volunteers, devoted families and skilled professionals who support persons with disabilities–and whose lives are touched by them in return.

Paralympics–Where Heroes Come is about the importance of trying. It's about reaching goals–and surpassing them. It is an inspiring story for all Albertans.

Shirley McClellan
Minister

INTRODUCTION

by Dr. Gary McPherson, Chairperson
Alberta Premier's Council on the Status of Persons with Disabilities

My introduction to the Paralympics was through the first Canadian Wheelchair Games, held at the University of Alberta in Edmonton in 1968. It was during that time that I met a young man, Robert Steadward. Little did I know that he would become the leader of the second biggest sport movement of the world, the International Paralympic Committee.

During the organization period for those games there was a postal strike, and as a ham radio operator I provided the communication link for the group. Bob Steadward, one of the key organizers, would come to our facility at the hospital every week and we would communicate with other parts of the country. That was my introduction to wheelchair sport. Three years later I became the president of the Paralympic Sports Association in Edmonton, which was really the first club with any sort of strength in the country. A lot of key people from that group went on to play significant roles in Canadian teams and internationally as well. I sort of grew up in the movement along with our current IPC president.

Back then I saw a certain development in the sport. We started from an institutional type of thinking where rehabilitation was really the purpose of wheelchair sport. The equipment being used was the old type of chairs, cumbersome and heavy, not designed for athletes. Then the equipment became more streamlined and more functional, and in the 90's became light weight, using titanium, aluminum, and different experimental combinations in terms of alloys. The progress of the equipment — not only wheelchairs but prosthetics — made the quality of competition accelerate at a great rate.

At the same time training methods were improving; we became less rehabilitative and more sport minded in our thinking, so more experienced coaches and trainers got involved. As a result athletes became much more focused. Instead of taking part in eight events, or five events, like we did when I first started, they would become specialists in one or two, be it marathoning, 800 metres, swimming, or whatever. We moved from a rehabilitative thinking and mode to a much more elite, competitive, committed type of athletic endeavour. The equipment went from low tech to very high tech, and the athletes, coaches, and trainers went from recreational to intensely competitive.

One area where we have not progressed as far as we would wish is in integration into able-bodied competition. In every Olympic Games since 1984, the men's 1500 metre and the women's 800 metre wheelchair races have been included, but only as demonstration events. The International Olympic Committee's acceptance of athletes with disabilities in full medal events would help the profile of disabled sport in those countries where the Olympics are represented, but the Paralympics are not.

The Paralympic Games show millions of disabled individuals around the world that they can achieve, and get recognition and respect for their efforts. The Paralympic movement is the second largest sport movement in the world, yet doesn't always get the media recognition, the corporate sponsorship, the profile, the funding, or the organizational backing necessary for success. Barcelona in 1992, where the Paralympics were intimately linked to the Olympics, and both sets of games were so well attended and so well organized, showed what can happen when the Paralympic movement receives the support it needs.

The whole disabled sport movement is about overcoming obvious limitations, and excelling at the same time. Paralympians include quality individuals from all over the world who could be role models for anyone anywhere, whether disabled or able bodied, male or female, young or old.

People involved in the Paralympics, right from the president on down, are volunteers who give their time and energy unselfishly to others. Paralympic athletes compete because they love the sport. Paralympic volunteers give so much of themselves because they love the sport, love the athletes, and love the environment. There are no fat pay cheques; when you win a gold medal you are not going to be an overnight sensation with the media, or get a huge corporate sponsorship.

People world wide are getting tired of corruption and dishonesty. They are attracted by the higher ideals and values of the Paralympics. The next challenge is to get the support from the public, corporate, government, and Olympic sectors that the Paralympic movement needs to maintain those ideals.

SECTION I: *History of the Paralympics*

*Dr. Robert Steadward, President of the International
Paralympic Committee, has committed his life to sport.
Why?*

*He says, "Sport has been a very important aspect of
my life because of the skills and lessons you learn from
sport, because of the various characteristics that it devel-
ops in you. It helps to form a philosophy of life. You grow
and mature with sport. You learn discipline from it. You
understand the concept of fair play, getting along with
people, competing in an environment of respect, working
with teammates."*

The Paralympics in Society

Certainly it has been shown in much research that, while sport has value in anyone's life, it is even more important in the life of a person with a disability. This is because of sport's rehabilitative influence, and the fact that it is a means to integrate the person into society.

Quite apart from the physiological benefits, sport teaches independence. Those who participate in sport find they are much more accepted in sports clubs, sports organizations, and by the community at large. As soon as the community sees the person with a disability participating in sports, that person is looked on as an equal member of society, not as an appendage or as someone different, but someone capable of achieving the same level of skills that a person without a disability can achieve.

In fact, nowadays people with disabilities participate not only in high-performance sport, but in competitive sport, recreational sport and lifetime activities that improve their overall fitness and lifestyle, so important for everyone. Sport

has also created an opportunity for people with disabilities to participate and be role models for others. It has opened doors for all people with disabilities to be a more integral part of society. Sport is vital to people with a disability because they have the same need to achieve as people without disabilities. Sport provides opportunities to showcase to the world just what disabled persons can achieve, thereby providing much-needed role models. Sport also provides opportunities for those with disabilities to take up the challenge to get fit, to become healthier, to look critically at their lifestyle, and to become equal contributors in society.

It's not surprising, given his philosophy, that Bob Steadward is the president of the second largest sport organization in the world. What is this Paralympic movement all about?

The Paralympics are often confused with the Special Olympics, where athletes with a mental handicap compete. Athletes with a mental handicap also compete in the Paralympics, but the focus of the Special Olympics is participation, not elite sport competition. All Paralympic athletes are elite athletes.

Like the Olympics, the Paralympic Games take place every two years, alternating summer and winter sports. The country hosting the Olympic Games also hosts the Paralympics, which immediately follow the Olympics. Events are Olympic events, or equivalents, with appropriate changes in

rules to allow for the functional ability of the athlete. The official aim of the Paralympic Games is "to unite competitors with a disability of all countries in fair and equal competition. No discrimination is allowed against any nation or person on the grounds of race, creed, religion, politics, or disability" (IPC, 1994).

The movement has grown dramatically since the first games in Rome in 1960. There 400 athletes with spinal cord injuries from 21 countries competed. In Atlanta in 1996, 103 countries sent 3195 elite athletes with disabilities including spinal cord injuries, visual impairment, cerebral palsy, limb amputations, those with a mental handicap, and les autres (athletes whose disabilities do not fit under the other categories). They competed in 19 sports. Their results in several instances compared very favourably with results achieved in the Olympic Games.

How did the Paralympics begin? Competitive sport for athletes with a disability is a relatively new phenomenon. It is generally agreed that the Paralympic movement towards competitive sports for individuals with a disability began in 1948 in Stoke Mandeville, United Kingdom.

Sir Ludwig Guttmann–
Father of the Paralympics

Sir Ludwig Guttmann, a neurosurgeon, began work at Stoke Mandeville Spinal Injuries Unit in 1944. Joan Scruton (later secretary general of the International Coordinating Committee, or ICC) became his secretary and assistant. She recalls the story Sir Ludwig told her about his inspiration. "In the first world war he was a medical orderly; he wasn't old enough to go in as a soldier. He said a patient was brought in, a big, strong man with a spinal cord injury, and they put him at the end of the ward. They put screens around him, saying there would really not be a need to go near him to treat his sores as he would be dead in a few months. Something in Sir Ludwig rebelled."

Dealing with limited resources, inexperienced staff, and this prevailing attitude that rehabilitation of patients with spinal cord injuries was impossible, Sir Ludwig looked for ways to inspire and integrate the ex-soldiers in his care back into society. Joan Scruton recalls that success did not come easily. "Some of these soldiers, or sailors, or airmen coming in from the battle-front were in terrible condition. Not only had they spinal cord injuries, but by the time they got to us they had terribly infected bedsores, kidney infection, and so forth."

As part of his innovative treatment program, Guttmann made work an everyday part of each patient's activities. He wanted his patients to resume normal life as quickly as possible. Given that most of his patients were young, formerly active individuals, sport was part of that normal life too.

Joan Scruton recalls, "One of the main treatments was sport, even when they were lying in bed. We had a quartermaster sergeant who was seconded from the army to do sport with the patients. When they were lying in bed he would throw a medicine ball to them and they would throw it back to get the strength in their arms."

Sir Ludwig realized that organized sports could work wonders in motivating patients to exercise, especially the young and formerly active war veterans he had in his care. Joan Scruton says, "Sport was of course critical to get their strength; their future depended on being able to lift themselves into the chair. The second point was psychological because when patients came in, they stayed sometimes three or four years to get over their sores and kidney infections and to rehabilitate."

Joan Scruton remembers how the sergeant and a patient started the first team sport: wheelchair polo. "They got in wheelchairs, and they had shortened sticks, and a disk for the puck, and they went up and down an empty ward hitting this puck. It was played against the physiotherapists, and later against the local football clubs." After some players received minor injuries in the fierce competition, polo was replaced by basketball, just as furious a sport but with less risk of damage.

Since Sir Ludwig made sport mandatory, it soon formed an essential part of the program at Stoke Mandeville. Miss Scruton recalls, "They had to do a sport. It was part of the treatment. It was not a question of would you like to do archery; no, it was part of the treatment, like taking their medicine, or doing physiotherapy. And Sir Ludwig would make sure that they did it."

Archery competition led to the first Stoke Mandeville Games for the Paralysed, held on July 28, 1948, and involving

16 competitors. It was no accident that these games opened on the same day as the Olympics. Sir Ludwig wanted his games to have a larger forum. He envisioned international games: Olympics

for athletes with disabilities. The Stoke Mandeville Games were held yearly after 1948, and became international in 1952 with the addition of a Dutch team of competitors. That same year the International Stoke Mandeville Games Federation, or ISMGF (later the International Stoke Mandeville Wheelchair Sports Federation, or ISMWSF) was created; it decided the games should be held in the country hosting the Olympics. And in 1960 in Rome, immediately after the Olympics, Sir Ludwig watched as 300 athletes entered the Olympic Stadium. From this has sprung the Paralympic Games, second in size only to the Olympics.

Instead of resting on his laurels, Sir Ludwig realized his work was just beginning. As president of the International Sports Organization for the Disabled (ISOD), founder of the

British Sports Association for the Disabled, and world-renowned expert in his professional field, he worked tirelessly to improve the day-to-day lives of those with disabilities. Sir Ludwig Guttmann passed away in 1980, having seen the influence of his games touch thousands of people worldwide. His vision continues to inspire all those who strive for his dream: the full integration of those with disabilities into mainstream society.

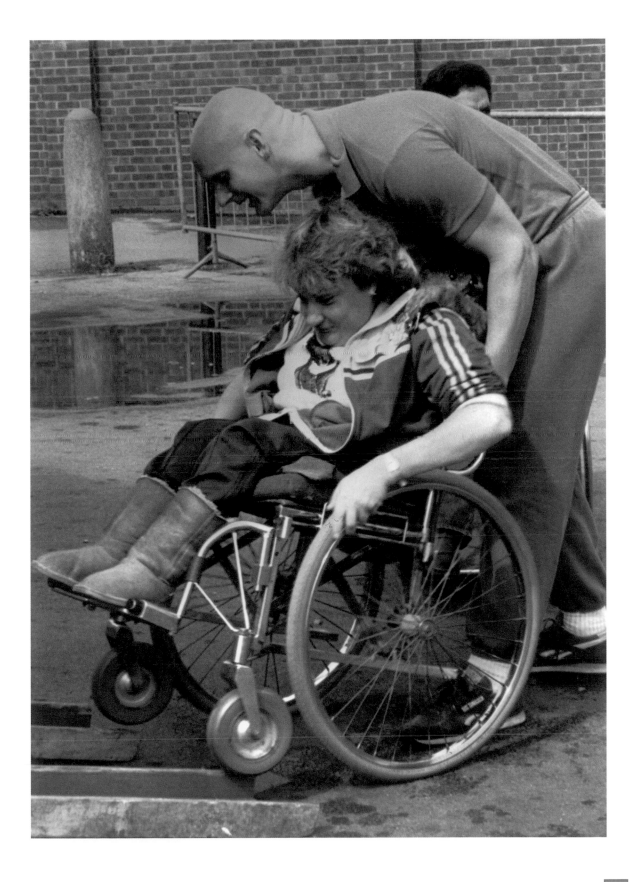

Paralympic Movement: 1960–88
From Rehabilitation to Elite Sport: The Metamorphosis

Between 1952 and 1970, although the international scope of the Stoke Mandeville Games grew and developed, it was still very much a medical model with a rehabilitation mentality. Nowhere was sport involved as we know it today. Dr. Steadward recalls, "My first exposure to Stoke Mandeville back in 1971 (the first time that Canada competed) was truly a shock to the system. Everyone for years had talked about Stoke Mandeville, and Sir Ludwig Guttmann being the grandfather of the Paralympic Games, and starting the Games there. We were looking for this magnificent sports structure but it was a great surprise.

"When we got there they had one small building, and in it was a little cafeteria, some offices that Sir Ludwig Guttmann and Joan Scruton worked out of, a small 25-metre pool, and a small gymnasium with a balcony for a couple of hundred fans. There were no facilities for track and field except an open field for throwing the javelin and discus. In 1971 they installed a new asphalt track which was a 100-metre-long straight-a-way with no lanes. The first 50 metres were uphill, and the next 50 metres were downhill. It wasn't until the mid 1970's that they started to build a 400-metre oval track, and an indoor lawn bowl centre, the Lady Guttmann Centre, named after Papa Guttmann's wife.

"The residences for the athletes and coaches were old wooden World War II huts. Each was one huge open building where there were 40 or 50 beds. There was no privacy whatsoever; at the other end of the hut was a bathroom that was an extension of where you slept, and a few cotton curtains to separate bath-tubs from toilets.

"As the cafeteria was quite small, the four hundred athletes there had to eat in several different shifts. All the food for years and years was TV dinners. Inmates from the local prison worked in the cafeteria kitchen, so it gave them a opportunity to get out and give some community service.

"There was no facility to encourage participants to so-cialise at the end of the day. Every night athletes would wheel down the roads of Stoke Mandeville going to the nearest pub for some fish and chips, to play darts, and have a few pints of beer. "

Gray Garner, photographer and former coach of the British Paralympic Wheelchair Basketball Team, recalls one of these pub trips. "The wheelies used to take a short cut through the hospital, but the gate they used was locked at 10:00 p. m. each night. This added a mile to the return trip. I used to drive to the pub and pick up the 'one-pointers,' and the rest used to hang on to the car bumper. At a very se-date pace, holding on to one another, they were towed back to Stoke Mandeville. One evening the police stopped me and very politely asked me if the gentlemen travelling behind were with me. Not knowing how many there were, I answered yes. They then asked me not to tow 17 wheelchairs on a main road at night without lights again!"

The 1972 Paralympic Games in Heidelberg, Germany, had a social tent, with lots of entertainment and food. Following this example, after the Stoke Mandeville people had build their 400 metre oval all-weather surface track, they put a tent over top of the old asphalt 100 metre track, and that became the entertainment tent every night. This kept the athletes in the village, because it was a great atmosphere.

Barb Montemurro, treasurer of the International Wheelchair Rugby Federation, took teams to Stoke many times. She recalls, "There was incredible camaraderie. I know a lot of the people complain about the food and the sleeping accommodations, but that's part of Stoke—part of the atmosphere. The other thing that was great about Stoke was that most of the venues were right there. Everybody could watch everybody else

compete in all the sports. At the big competition like the Paralympics that is very difficult to do. "

Dr. Steadward recalls a significant change. "After the attack on the Israeli athletes at the 1972 Munich Olympics, security was of great concern for the Stoke organisers. In 1973 they created a special village for the Israeli team. In order to try to ensure that it was made as safe as possible, they put a few of the heads of delegations from different countries with the Israeli team in a little agricultural college about a mile up the road from Stoke Mandeville. We had to have very strict identification on us at all times, and we were searched and asked questions every time we came in and out of the residence there. There were police patrols going around the building 24 hours a day, with dogs and guns.

"I remember one particular night I came back from the tent where the socialising was going on, and I forgot my pack sack with my identification in it, and the security guard, even though he knew me from the previous year, wouldn't let me in, so I had to spend the night outside talking with him. That particular village had to stay in place for a number of years during the 70's and the 80's. We used to refer to it as our little Israeli Kibbutz; we became really close friends with the Israeli team and a number of their staff. So there were lots of interesting experiences back in the old Stoke Mandeville days. "

Stoke Mandeville was of course not the only place in the world where disabled sport competitions were held. The Comité International des Sports des Sourds (CISS), was established in 1924 to organise international games for deaf athletes. These competitions, modelled on the Olympic Games, grew into the World Games for the Deaf, and are held every four years.

Other disabled sport organisations followed. The First National Wheelchair Basketball Tournament was held in the United States in 1949, followed by the National Wheelchair Games in 1957. While the ISMWGF limited participants to those with spinal injuries, the American organisations wel-

comed competitors with any type of lower body impairment. This early disparity was to lead to friction between Guttmann and those who advocated that anyone who could play the sport should be allowed to compete. Guttmann maintained that competition should only occur between those with similar disabilities. His opponents argued that competition should occur between those who could do the sport equally well, no matter the type of disability.

The sport approach was to prevail at the outset in Winter Games. Hans Lindström, IPC technical officer, one of the organisers recalls, "We were not controlled by the disability orientation that Sir Ludwig and the summer sports had. What we could create was a system for winter sports which was fair, and based on sports, not on disabilities."

There was to be more disagreement between Guttmann and others in the movement. André Raes, organiser of the first European Wheelchair Basketball Championship, recalls Guttmann's opposition to the idea of organising a world championship for wheelchair basketball anywhere but at Stoke Mandeville. As a result of Raes's success in organising international tournaments, Guttmann invited him to the Stoke Mandeville Games in July, 1972, where the Wheelchair Section of the ISMGF was set up, with Raes as its first chairman. This led to the establishment in 1973 of the Gold Cup Wheelchair Basketball World Championships.

The International Games for the Disabled in Tokyo in 1964 saw the first wheelchair races, which were held as demonstration events. The first games ever to include disabilities other than spinal cord were the Winter Games held in 1976 in Örnsköldsvik, Sweden, for blind, amputee and athletes with spinal cord injuries. Later that year in Toronto the list of Summer Games competitors included the blind, amputees and les autres athletes for the first time in Paralympic history. In 1980, Arnhem, Netherlands saw athletes with cerebral palsy in Paralympic competition for the first time. The Winter Games in 1980 were held in Geilo, Norway.

By this time there were a number of different disabled sport organisations involved in the games. In order to deal with organisational problems, and because the International Olympic Committee (IOC) wanted to deal with a single body in its negotiations regarding disabled sport, the International Coordinating Committee of World Sports Organisations for the Disabled (ICC) was formed in 1983.

While the ICC was a huge step forward in the development of disabled sport world-wide, it was not without its problems. Members were appointed, not elected, there was no national representation in the organisation, and the sport federations refused to allow their athletes to participate in each others' events. Nevertheless, the ICC accomplished much during its 12 years of existence.

In 1984 the Summer Games were split due to problems with funding and organisation. Two Games were held: one at Stoke Mandeville for the paralysed, and one at New York for amputees, the blind, and those with cerebral palsy. The Winter Games were held in Innsbruck, Austria for all locomotor disabilities. In addition, athletes were involved in giant sla-

lom and three track skiing as demonstration events at the Olympics in Sarajevo.

The moment heralding the birth of the International Paralympic Committee took place in Arnhem in 1987. Representatives voted to change the structure of the ICC to include not only representation from the sport federations, but also regional and athlete representation.

The 1988 Seoul Paralympics dramatically demonstrated the effects of proper organisation, and the shift in the disabled sport community from sport as rehabilitation, to sport as recreation, to elite sport. New methods of training for athletes, coaches and officials made these games successful. The winning athlete was the elite athlete, one at the peak of training and conditioning. Thus these Games are considered the first games of the modern Paralympic era.

The International Paralympic Committee was founded on September 21, 1989 in Dusseldorf (Federal Republic of Germany) by the six international organisations representing sport for the disabled, and the nations attending the Inaugural General Assembly. The existing international federations were

- CISS: Comité International des Sports des Sourds
- CP-ISRA: Cerebral Palsy International Sport and Recreation Association
- IBSA: International Blind Sports Association
- INAS-FMH: International Association Sport for Persons with Mental Handicap
- ISMGF: International Stoke Mandeville Games Federation, which later became

• ISOD: International Sports Organisation for the Disabled

The assembly voted unanimously that the International Paralympic Committee would be the sole world governing body for athletes with a disability. While the federations continue to administer their individual sport disability groups, the IPC organises all world championships, Paralympic trials, and Paralympic Games.

Later CISS withdrew from the IPC, which has agreed that Games organised by CISS for athletes with hearing impairment have status equal to that of the Paralympic Games.

The IPC official logo evolved from the five teardrop logo of the 1988 Seoul Paralympics, which was based on the symbol of yin and yang. The IOC objected to this logo, saying it was too similar to the Olympic five rings, and threatened to withdraw all support if it were not changed. In the interest of creating harmony between the two organisations, the IPC reduced the tear drops to three to match the three words of the motto: "Mind, Body, Spirit," the philosophy which was to lead the organisation into its next great phase.

International Paralympic Games: Summer

YEAR	LOCATION	DISABILITIES INCLUDED	NUMBER OF COUNTRIES	NUMBER OF ATHLETES	SHARED VENUES WITH OLYMPICS	HIGHLIGHTS
1952	Stoke Mandeville	Spinal cord injury	2	130	No	First international games for disabled
1960	Rome, Italy	Spinal cord injury	23	400	Yes	First games for disabled held in same venue as Olympic games.
1964	Toyko, Japan	Spinal cord injury	22	390	Yes	Wheelchair racing added
1968	Tel Aviv, Israel	Spinal cord injury	29	750	No	
1972	Heidelburg, Germany	Spinal cord injury	44	1000	No	First quadriplegic competition added; demonstration events for visually impaired
1976	Toronto, Canada	Spinal cord injury Visually impaired Les autres	42	1600	No	First use of specialized racing wheelchairs
1980	Arnhem, Holland	Spinal cord injury Amputee Visually impaired Cerebral Palsy	42	2500	No	

International Paralympic Games: Summer (continued)

YEAR	LOCATION	DISABILITIES INCLUDED	NUMBER OF COUNTRIES	NUMBER OF ATHLETES	SHARED VENUES WITH OLYMPICS	HIGHLIGHTS
1984	Stoke Mandeville, UK & New York, USA	Spinal cord injury Amputee Visually impared Cerebral Palsy	42	4080	No	Wheelchair marathon introduced
1988	Seoul, Korea	Spinal cord injury	61	3053	Yes	Commitment made by the Olympic Organizing Committee to assist the Paralympic Committee Cycling
1992	Barcelone, Spain	Spinal cord injury Amputee Visually impaired Cerebral Palsy Les Autres	82	3020	Yes	Event yet unsurpassed in organizational excellence
1996	Atlanta, USA	Spinal cord injury Amputee Visually impaired Cerebral Palsy Les Autres Mentally Handicapped	103	3195	Yes	First world-wide sponsors

International Paralympic Games: Winter

YEAR	LOCATION	DISABILITIES INCLUDED	NUMBER OF COUNTRIES	NUMBER OF ATHLETES	SHARED VENUES WITH OLYMPICS	HIGHLIGHTS
1976	Örnsköldsvik, Sweden	Blind amputee	14	250+	No	Demonstration event: sledge racing
1980	Geilo, Norway	All locomotor disabilities	18	350+	No	Demonstration event: Sledge down-hill racing
1984	Innsbruck, Austria	All locomotor disabilities	22	350+	No	Demonstration event at Olympics in Sarajevo: giant slalom; three track skiers
1988	Innsbruck, Austria	All locomotor disabilities	22	397	No	Athletes from USSR; sit-skiing introduced as event in alpine and nordic
1992	Tignes-Albertville, France	All locomotor disabilities	24	475	Yes	Demonstration event: alpine and cross-country skiing for athletes with mental disabilities
1994	Lillehammer, Norway	All locomotor disabilities	31	1000+	Yes	Sledge hockey introduced

SECTION II: *The Modern Paralympics*

Summer Games The Sophisticated Games

Seoul, 1988: "United for the Challenge"

"The Land of the Morning Calm"

The Seoul organising committee used a variation on rent-a-crowd to fill the stadium and other venues. Empty seats would have been discouraging, so tickets were given to different community groups: church groups, Boy Scouts, Girl Guides, college groups, sport club groups; all sorts of people came in groups, creating a very good atmosphere.

The athletes were thrilled to perform in front of full-capacity, highly appreciative crowds. School children were organised to support teams from various countries, so a class would show up dressed in the colours of one team and cheer them on to victory.

Elaine Ell, Canadian wheelchair basketball player, recalls, "In Seoul you really felt like you were at the Olympics because the crowd was so well organised. We played in front of 20,000 people for the bronze medal match. At the Opening Ceremonies we marched in front of 100,000 people. There was great excitement among the athletes at those Games because of all the different disciplines included—wheelchair, cerebral palsy, visually impaired were all together."

One characteristic of the Seoul Games was their military precision. Every aspect of the games was imbued with military control, beginning with arrival at the airport, where athletes were greeted by well-armed soldiers. Security continued to be tight: all the vehicles used to transport participants were checked daily for bombs. As people entered or exited venues, their bags and

parcels were searched. While this was an odd sensation for those used to the rather more casual atmosphere in other countries, it did give participants the sense they were being protected.

The Seoul Games were truly world class. After the debacle of 1984, the Seoul organising committee's scrupulous attention to detail ensured a successful

competition. Many of the officials had honed their skills at the Olympic Games. Athletes were housed in a specially-constructed village designed to be used after the games by individuals with disabilities. Official transport was efficient and

prompt, although there were horrendous traffic tie-ups at times.

Because of the cost and limited availability of Olympic Opening Ceremonies tickets, the organising committee decided that they would put on exactly the same Opening Ceremonies for the Paralympic Games so that the local people in Korea would have an opportunity to attend. The Opening Ceremonies were spectacular: skydivers, jets flying past, thousands of children, a T'aekwondo demonstration, stunning Korean dances, and

700 wheelchair dancers. The moment many found most moving was the circuit of the last torch bearer, Cho Hyun-hee, in a wheelchair pushed by her daughter, Yum Bo-ram.

Ljiljana Ljubisic, double medallist in discus and javelin, recalls her feelings about Seoul. "In 1984 we

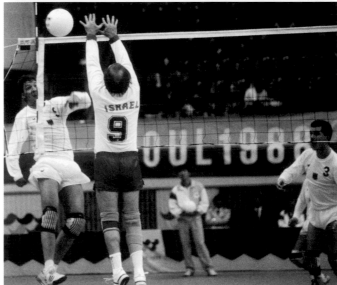

were at least in decent accommodations. They were clean. The food was excellent. It was fabulous. The venues for competitions were of a standard that were equivalent to a state college in the United States, but the feeling, the camaraderie, the pageantry; that was where the essence of why we were there was intact. In Korea we went another step higher. We had a Paralympic Village, and we were in the same city, in the same country as the Olympics. That was a huge step in our identity and our ability to raise money in order to do what we needed to do. Seoul was a big step forward because we were now the true Paralympic Games and we were parallel with the Olympics and we were in the same city and so forth. It was like wow—competing in the same stadium and on the same turf as Ben Johnson, and having food and facilities available to us that were required."

But Seoul had its problems too; due to a shortage of housing, only 3000 athletes were able to attend the

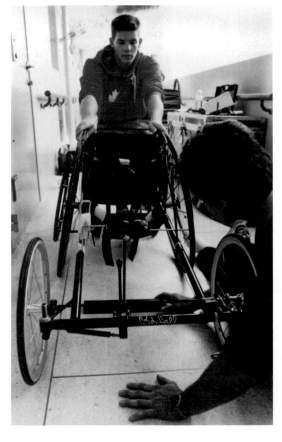

games. This limited the number of competitors. There were also some technical problems. Pat Heydon, director of Games Missions, Canadian Paralympic Committee, recalls, "While we had come of age in terms of holding the games in the same city and using some of the venues, we still hadn't achieved the milestone of having that technical credibility. For example, when the athletes are in the pool, you've got to remember that if they are supposed to touch with two hands, they are supposed to touch with two hands; it doesn't matter if they are disabled or not. The athletes want to be called on those things, and they are the first to tell you when technically the games are not sound. So that was a particular challenge."

The organising committee made a number of last-minute decisions to eliminate many events involving severely disabled athletes, those events where

fewer than three athletes were entered. The problem was not with the decision to cancel the events; the problem was with the timing of those decisions. Countries were not notified far enough in advance so that the athletes had the option to challenge athletes in a tougher class so that they still got an opportunity to go to the games. The decision to reduce the number of events was a symptom of the change these games represented: the Paralympic athlete must be the elite athlete.

And elite they truly were: there was Trischa Zorn, with 12 gold medals in swimming and nine world records. There was Connie Hansen, with five gold medals in wheelchair racing. In all, 971 new world records were set. The modern Paralympic era had begun.

Logistics: *

Participating Countries	61
Athletes	3053
Officials	305
Referees	554
Escorts	962
International organisation members	100
Media personnel	2368
Seoul Paralympic Organizing Committee (SPOC) members	248
Volunteers	6431
Assistants	4971
Temporary employees	73
Performers in ceremonies	12,156
World records set	971
Events	729
Demonstration events	2
Cost	$26,000,000

*All statistics are taken from the Official Report.

Barcelona, 1992: "Sport Without Limits"

D r. Steadward recalls, "The atmosphere in Barcelona was absolutely wonderful. The Spanish people love to have a party, love to have a good time, and it was a wonderful experience and great atmosphere. Who could imagine a better village than a brand-new housing complex right on the Mediterranean Sea? Organisers provided a wonderful cafeteria, excellent rooms to live in, exceptionally good offices for the teams, and a great wind-up party for the athletes where they brought in the top bands. The atmosphere was likely the best that we have ever experienced in Summer Games.

"Barcelona is still one of the greatest mysteries of the world today to me. People don't normally go to free events, but we played to packed houses. There were line-ups outside the venues for hours and hours to get the best seats in the house."

Athletes were in no doubt that people came because they wanted to come, and stayed because they were thrilled by what they saw. And they saw greatness. An astounding number of records were broken.

Ljiljana Ljubisic recalls, "Being surrounded by hundreds of young kids treating you like a superstar was a first for us. There were adults, not even children, but adults, asking for your autograph, or your photograph, and wishing to trade a pin or something with you. It was tremendous."

A new functional classification system was developed for the Barcelona Games in 1992. Classification began more than a year before the games, with specialists working to classify 2200 of the athletes. That left 1180 to be processed at the classification centre. The number of classes were considerably reduced, so that there were some events cancelled, but the new classifications did result in greater numbers of athletes in the various sports, which provided better competition for the athletes and also avoided the cancellation of a lot of events.

Because the organising committee was closely linked to the Olympic organising committee, standards

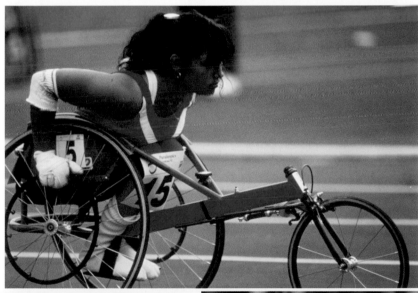

in all areas were very high. This was a far cry from the early days when the poorest sorts of conditions were endured by athletes with a disability. In Barcelona, as in Seoul, elite athletes were given elite treatment.

The Opening Ceremonies were a marvel of art and organisation, from the Picasso-inspired masks given to spectators, to the Gothic cathedral backdrop, to the flamenco dancers and horsemen, all reflecting the Spanish love for their culture and traditions. A spectacular feat was when the mascot, who was an armless person, rode a motorcycle up a series of ramps right up to the peak of the stadium.

In his address to the athletes, Stephen Hawking, the renowned physicist who has made immeasureable contributions to science despite battling an incurable neuromuscular disease, addressed the athletes. He said, "Each one has within us the spark of fire, a creative torch." His words echoed in the climactic moment when the archer shot the flaming arrow, which went right out of the stadium, up on top of the cauldron, and lit the Paralympic torch.

As in Seoul, thousands of people participated in the Barcelona Games. Daily extensive television coverage ensured that all Spain and much of Europe shared in the excitement. ONCE, the national lottery owned totally by the blind, paid for and marketed the games, providing approximately 75 million dollars. The atmosphere, participation and attendance achieved in Barcelona set a standard for all future Paralympics.

Ljiljana Ljubisic recalls, "The biggest difference in Barcelona was the people. It was their acceptance and regard of athletes with disabilities. They saw no difference between the able-bodied person and the athlete with a disability. When it came to performance, we were equivalent to the Olympics. It was the first time that we were treated 100% fully like the athletes that we are and respected as the human beings that we are, and there was no difference in attitude, or facility, or access to facility and programs, and that is what made Barcelona the most fabulous Paralympic Games."

Reinhild Moller, winter and summer medallist, sums up the attitude in Barcelona with this anecdote. "I was watching the amputee high jump. There was one official standing there and every time an athlete started hopping towards the high jump, this official was hopping with him. He was so with the athlete; he was, with his whole body, wanting to lift the athlete over the pole. I thought, *Here are all these able-bodied people really trying to cheer us on and support us.*"

Seoul had inspired athletes, coaches and sports manufacturers to new heights. These advances in training, coaching and sport technology led to wonderful performances in Barcelona. Times and distances in those events also included in the Olympics were closer than ever. One example was Ajibola Adeoye of Nigeria, a single-arm amputee, who ran the 100m in 10.72 seconds. Another was Tony Volpentest, using two prostheses, who ran 100 metres in 11.63 seconds, only 1.77 slower than Carl Lewis' record of 9.86.

Trischa Zorn, USA, shone again, winning 10 gold medals in swimming. Her team-mate, John Morgan, won eight gold

and two silver; Joanne Mucz of Canada won five gold. The Canadian women's wheelchair basketball team fought a glorious match, defeating USA 35-26, led by star Chantal Benoit, who scored 18 points.

Of course these games were not without controversy. In addition to the event cancellations, there were three instances of doping. Two athletes were stripped of silver medals for anabolic steroid use; the US basketball team was stripped of their gold medal because one player used an analgesic narcotic.

But the legacy left by the Barcelona Games is impressive. The urban renewal of Barcelona resulted in the building of one thousand specially designed apartments that were barrier-free and incorporated many features for ease of use by those with disabilities.

The first Paralympic Congress ever was held, bringing together sport

professionals from around the world to discuss issues relating to sport for athletes with disabilities. Delegates agreed that education, media awareness and government support were key to the movement's continued success.

Logistics*:

Volunteers	8000+
Television viewers	7 million
Total public attendance	2,372,650
Athletes	3020
Countries	82
Officials, referees, judges, assistants	659
Events	489
COOB staff	12,000+
Total cost	9,527.9 million pesetas
World records set	279
Official sponsors and suppliers	36

*All statistics are taken from the Official Report.

Atlanta, 1996: "The Triumph of the Human Spirit"

There were three major milestones in Atlanta. First, there was stellar achievement: more athletes, from more countries setting more world records, than ever before. These games included, for the first time, athletes with a mental handicap. This inclusion had met with some opposition, especially from the host organising committee.

Bernard Atha of the International Sports Federation for Persons with Mental Handicap says, "When the Paralympics first started, they were only for wheelchair athletes with spinal injuries. When the blind first came in, there was opposition to the blind. There still is. There are some who say, 'Look, if a blind person can run without a guide, why should he or she be in the Paralympics?' Then the next one to come in were the people with cerebral palsy, and there was enormous opposition to them. The world of sport with people with disabilities agreed that there would be one world, not several different worlds, and so mentally handicapped as a disability falls properly within the world of sport for disabled people. It is just a different disability from the blind, and a different disability from a person who a lost a limb. But it is a disability in just the same way, and therefore they have every right to be part of the movement. If that right were denied, it would be

a discrimination which nobody supporting people with disabilities in society could tolerate."

A second milestone was the major involvement of world-wide and national sponsors using the Paralympics as an investment opportunity rather than as a charitable deduction. There were over 60 formal contracts signed with different companies around the United States that provided cash or value in kind to support the games. For the first time sponsors were classified into different categories depending on the amount of cash or value in kind provided to the organising committee. There were four world-wide sponsors: Coca Cola, IBM, Motorola, Turner Broadcasting. There were a number of official sponsors such as Kodak, Swatch, Home Depot, Sunrise, Bell South, and Naya Spring Water.

The third major achievement of the Atlanta Games was the involvement for the first time of a quasi-host broadcaster that provided television feed for the various countries around the world. The only difficulty was that most of the coverage was on American athletes, so it was very difficult for other countries to get good feed that covered their own athletes.

While Atlanta saw major achievements in a number of areas, there were also major problems. Dr. Steadward says, "The volunteers associated with the Games were wonderful: they were kind, proud, enthusiastic and supportive. They could not do

enough for us. But I was really disappointed that the American public did not purchase more tickets, and show their commitment and their enthusiasm for the athletes who were there participating in the Games.

"As well, I was extremely frustrated and saddened by the lack of support and co-operation from the Atlanta Olympic organising committee. To me, they were very egotistical and showed very little, if any support for the Atlanta Paralympic Organising Committee (APOC). That was why a number of the venues were in such poor condition when the Paralympic organising committee took them over, and why we had such a tremendous difficulty with the Athletes' Village as well."

Breaking new ground is apt to have its problems, and the new level of sponsorship at the Paralympics was no exception. Steadward says, "Advertising on uniforms was abused, and as a result, created problems with some of the sponsors, and so we have a lot of mending to do in the future. Some of the nations broke the advertising rules. For example, some of the wheelchair basketball teams had spoke-protector logos from

sponsors that were in direct conflict with Sunrise Medical, a major sponsor who gave a substantial amount of money for exclusivity. That created problems for IPC, problems for the organising committee, and provided an unfortunate set of circumstances around wheelchair basketball."

Another problem was with visibility of the IPC logo. Steadward says, "When you go to the Olympic Games you see those five rings everywhere. You see it in the organising committee's logo, you see it at every venue, on every flag pole: the entire town is decorated by the IOC logo. But in Atlanta you saw very little evidence of the IPC logo, whether with sponsors, with advertising, in the venues, or anywhere. The organising committee made no effort to ensure that our logo was clearly visible around the city, and made an integral part of the Atlanta Games."

Dr. Steadward narrowly averted what could have been a major public embarrassment for the Atlanta Paralympic organising committee. He recalls, "The athletes were so angry with regards to the village: the lack of bedding, the dirty accommodation, food line-ups or no food, and all sorts of problems there, that they were going to hold a protest at the Closing Ceremonies. This would have been quite a spectacle and public embarrassment for the host organising committee. I only found out about the protest 20 minutes before I was going down to make a speech at the Closing Ceremonies. I had people go down onto the field and bring back to me the athletes who were leading this protest.

'It wasn't that I didn't support the athletes. But I wanted to talk to them to say 'Look at it this way. The Games from a point of view of what you as athletes have achieved is spectacular. You have provided great entertainment and some great thrills for us; let's not spoil it and put a black mark against yourselves in these Games by putting on this public demonstration against the organising committee, the city of Atlanta, and the USA.'

"I convinced them not to have the protest, but did promise them that I would take their protest banner to our next executive committee meeting, hang it in the meeting, take a picture of it with the executive board, and then publish it in our next IPC newsletter."

Some involved in the Atlanta Games had very positive experiences. Pawel Zbieranowski, chairman of the International Wheelchair Rugby Federation, says, "We were very, very pleased with Atlanta. The rugby tournament went very well. There were some little things that had to be done at the last moment, but that is to be expected. Overall the Games, from a sport point of view, were a great success."

Marie-Claire Ross, winner of six medals in swimming, says, "Atlanta was a huge celebration of sport, of life, of everything. Even on the bad days, even when people had a bad swim or were disappointed with their achievements, you weren't upset. It was still just overwhelmingly positive. I met so many wonderful people from all sorts of countries. There were things about Atlanta that were sort of disheartening: the lack of coverage internation-

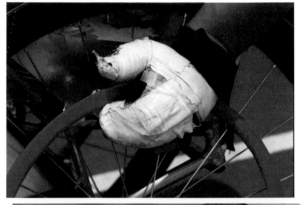

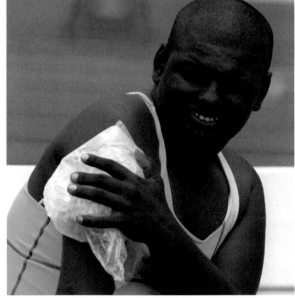

ally, and also the downsizing from the Olympics to the Paralympics, but these didn't dampen the spirits, I don't think, of the people participating. I realised, again, every single hour that I was there, it was a special time and I just made the most of it."

Chris Cohen, chairman of the IPC Athletic Committee, and technical delegate both to Barcelona and Atlanta, was very impressed by the calibre of the Atlanta volunteers and the sport professionalism. But he had strong feelings about the organisational problems that made his job much more difficult than it should have been. In his technical delegate's report, compiled in September 1996, Cohen writes, "I saw the terrible state of the stadium, the technology and the services after the close of the Olympics. I have never seen such devastation brought about by anyone other than vandals, certainly never by employees doing a job for which they were obviously being paid. This was the cost of separation of organising committees, more than in any other area."

Onc example of this was the cabling needed for the computers in the Olympic Stadium. Cohen says, "I was talking to one man who was laying the optic fibre for the photo-finish system for the Paralympics; they used the same wiring for the Olympics but it had all been cut out by the television company. He was laying the cable and every time he went to test it on one particular morning, it would work for a few seconds and then it just stopped. When he followed the wire back, he found the worker from the television company cutting the wires as he was laying them."

In some ways Atlanta was doomed by its own success. Problems encountered by athletes, officials and media were partly a result of the enormous numbers of participants. Gray Garner, photographer for the *London Times* newspaper and 30-year veteran of disabled sport events, found it almost impossible to do his job. Promised full access to media facilities, he recalls, "When I get out there I find that I'm in competition with college students, with people from wheelchair firms, with limb-fitting centres, all of which have been given full accreditation. So

instead of 50-odd photographers, we are now dealing with 450-500, which swelled every day; there were more and more and more. Consequently it was an absolute nightmare to even try to get on the track. I managed it twice in 10 days."

But despite its problems, Atlanta saw stellar achievement: 269 new world records were set.

*Logistics

Participating countries	103
Athletes	3195
Volunteers	11,344
Military personnel (workers)	1000
APOC staff members	10,000+
Media representatives (accredited)	1661
Cost	$90 million
Official sponsors (giving from $2,000,000 to $6,000,000)	25
New World Records set	269
Judges/officials	780
Official donors (giving from $10,000 to $1,000,000)	25+
Events	517
Delegation staff	1717

* All statisitcs taken from official report.

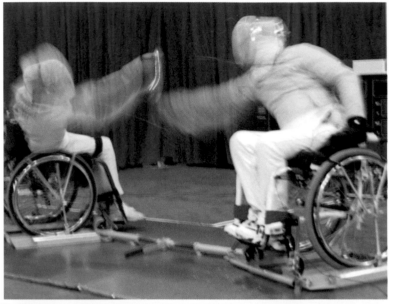

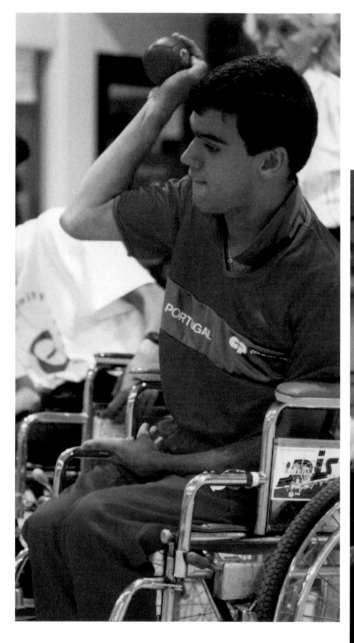

Developing Sports
for the Summer Paralympics

As the world disabled sport movement grows, new sports develop, and other sports decline in use. These changes are reflected in the sports that the International Paralympic Committee include in the Paralympic Games. Different guidelines are used for summer and winter sports, but to be included, a new sport must be widely practised around the world. It must be played by men in at least 15 countries and on three continents, or by women in at least 10 countries and on three continents. The sport must be administered by a recognised sport organisation A constitution and classification system must be established so that all of the aspects of the administration of the sport are in place. World championships must be held that involve at least 50 percent of the countries that participate in the sport. Application for admission must be made years in advance, and a careful screening process done to ensure that the sport will be a successful part of Paralympic competition.

Wheelchair rugby was a demonstration sport in Atlanta, but is now a Paralympic event. Pawel Zbieranowski, chairman of the Rugby Section of ISMWSF and president of the International Wheelchair Rugby Federation, reflects on this development. "We had to make a presentation at an IPC meeting. The proposal is looked at by their committee, and they decide if all the criteria are fulfilled to their liking; then it happens. If not, then somebody has to do a bit more homework. Actually, that is what happened to us in '94; we made, I would think, a pretty good presentation, but they found some grey areas where they wanted some more information, and the following year we were successful.

"Being involved in rugby we have experienced the impact of being in the Paralympics for quite a while. It is an interesting situation. All the new patients turning into athletes—people after their accidents—the first sort of sport-related activity that they usually come across is rugby. A number of these people got involved in rugby and started playing, and when they really taste a sport as such, then they want to go somewhere higher than just the national championships or international tournaments. Rugby was not able to provide them with the possibility to go the Paralympics, so we lost a number of tremendous athletes who switched to sports like athletics, or tennis, or swimming, or shooting, and went to the Paralympics. So you can see that the meaning of Paralympics was very high and they were willing to sacrifice one sport for another in order to go to those games. So now with us coming to the Paralympics, and sort of competing with other sports on the equal level, now there is a situation where some of the former rugby athletes are coming back to us. Or those who were involved in other sports are switching to us. So I would say it created a more healthy situation, but the meaning is just tremendous. Everybody talks about Olympians, watching them on TV, and now these people can do the same and experience the same feelings.

"But the recognition we received from the other athletes and countries at the Atlanta Paralympics was tremendous. The most recent example is that the Far East and South Pacific Re-

gion Federation has asked us for rules and the classification system we use, and for educational materials about rugby because they learned about rugby in Atlanta and they would like to start it in their region. So that is sort of an example that rugby had.

"The interesting thing is that since Atlanta there have been some changes made in the IPC regulations; for instance, there won't be any more demonstration sports; sports will go directly to the medal sport status. I pushed quite a bit for this. We have to fulfil the same criteria as the sports that are already medal sports, so it doesn't seem to be sensible to have a demonstration sport step when you still have to have the same criteria as the medal sports. So that was scrapped; whoever comes next will be able to jump directly into it. The other change was that we changed the criteria for sports to be recognised as Paralympic. The number of countries being 15 was very discriminating against the team sports, because if you take an individual sport you might have five athletes in a particular country and you can successfully run a national championship, so virtually what you would need would be 75 athletes in some sports to become an official Paralympic sport. Then you look at the team sport, where you need four or five teams to run a national championship, and that is already 50 athletes in one country. It makes it very awkward and difficult to join. So the limits were lowered for team sports to 12, and individual sports were put up to 18 to counterbalance the overall situation."

Bob Lowe, chairman of the Lawn Bowls Committee, faces a different scenario. Lawn bowls has been dropped from the Paralympic program for the 2000 Games in Sydney, because fewer than the required 18 countries agreed to hold national competitions in lawn bowls. The IPC feels that it is a Commonwealth sport rather than a Paralympic sport.

Lowe vigorously disagrees, saying that a number of Asian countries have recently taken up the sport. He is particularly disappointed that the sport will not be played in Sydney. He says, "Lawn bowls is one of the most followed sports in the Paralympics; 50 percent of the Australians play the game of lawn bowls, and unfortunately it cannot go ahead."

CHAPTER 6

Winter Games —
The Family Games

While the Summer Games are huge, the Winter Games are still small, intimate events with a family atmosphere. Most of the participants know one another well, and the logistics for the organising committee are much less complicated. The other major difference is that the Winter Paralympics were started by people with a sport rather than a medical background, and so they have always operated on the basis of functional classification.

They are organised according to athletes' physical ability to do the sport, rather than on their medical diagnosis.

Winter sports for the disabled present obvious difficulties; problems of transport and equipment are aggravated by cold, ice and snow. But these games still doubled in size between 1976 and 1994: while Sweden hosted 15 countries in '76, Norway hosted 31 in '94. The addition of new sports such as short-track ice sledge racing, as well as the development in training regimens and equipment, will ensure this growth continues.

Tignes-Albertville 1992

Tignes-Albertville included only skiing events; ice sports such as sledge racing and hockey were not included, as no facilities for these were available. Athletes with mental disabilities participated in Winter Paralympics for the first time, doing demonstration events in alpine and cross-country skiing.

Logistics*

Participating countries	24
Athletes	475
Volunteers	450
Military personnel	90
Media representatives	300
Budget	70,000,000 francs
Official sponsors	5

*All statistics are taken from the Official Report.

*Hans Lindström says, "Lillehammer was the
best ever: good weather, good people, good
competition, remarkable performances."*

Lillehammer, 1994

Pat Heydon contrasts Tignes with Lillehammer. "It's the whole coming of age of the Paralympic Games: you go from Tignes to Lillehammer, and Lillehammer was just wonderful by comparison."

Dr. Gudrun Doll-Tepper, disabled sport historian and researcher, believes Lillehammer was a milestone. "Lillehammer was really a huge step forward because the public and the media had so much interest. Then there was the introduction of new

sports. I remember so well the first time I saw an ice sledge hockey game. People were really shouting; they were so excited to see such a new game. It opened doors to those who are only interested in sport in general, but not so much in disability sport. Lillehammer in that respect made a great contribution to the whole movement."

This was the first Paralympic Games organised by the newly formed International Paralympic Committee, since previous Games contracts had been signed with the ICC. By all standards, Lillehammer was a resounding success. Much of this was due to co-operation in planning: Gerhard Heiberg was president of both the Lillehammer Olympic Organising Committee (LOOC) and the Lillehammer Paralympic Organising Committee (LPOC). Although their original plan to stage the Olympics and Paralympics simultaneously had to be abandoned due to problems of logistics, Norway's clearly demonstrated commitment to the success of both events resulted in superb organisation and stellar achievement. Dr. Steadward says, "There was one president in charge of both Games, but more important were the warmth, and friendliness, and heart of the Norwegian people who came out and supported all of the athletes of ice and snow from around the world."

This commitment was demonstrated in many different ways. The king and queen of Norway were in attendance almost daily. Media coverage of the games was unprecedented for a winter event. Norwegian television prepared daily 55-minute reports. This footage was bought by 27 television stations from 17 countries.

Logistics:

Participating countries	31
Athletes	1000+
Volunteers	550
Military personnel -workers	350
LPOC staff members	18
Media representatives	650
Budget	$12 million
Official sponsors	3 main; 9 total

The Paralympic Village in Lillehammer was home to all the participants: team members, volunteers, administration, performers, technical personnel, and the LPOC staff.

Opening Ceremonies were held in Hakon's Hall. Highlights included wheelchair dancing, Norwegian folk dancing, and performers from around the world.

The Alpine courses on Hafjell were incredibly tough: at times icy, and always fast. But the endurance and expertise of many competitors proved yet again that the Paralympic athlete is the elite athlete. And the disabled athlete obviously faces a much tougher job than the able-bodied; witness the blind skiing events where the competitor not only deals with a challenging course, but also with the challenges specific to disability, such as the blind skier's guide looking back to check on progress, falling and also taking the competitor down. Or having the guide's auditory signals drowned out by the noise of the cheering crowd: some events had several thousand spectators.

Some obstacles weren't part of the competition. Pat Heydon recalls, "There are a lot of other hazards too. I can remember that they tried to beautify the area and they had planters spaced around. Unfortunately they kept moving them around every day. One of our blind athletes who was walking unguided with a cane missed tapping the box, fell over, and broke one of his wrists. He hadn't competed at that point yet."

Sledge hockey, the Paralympic version of ice hockey, was a new event in Lillehammer, and spectators loved it. Kristin's Hall was another venue that was often full of cheering fans ready to embrace this event. Tickets were so hard to get that they were being scalped. Another first: the Norwegian team included a female goalie.

Norwegians collected most of the gold medals in this most successful Winter Paralympics ever. The organisers of the 1998 Nagano Winter Games will be hard-pressed to measure up to the national spirit, support and commitment poured into Lillehammer by the Norwegian people.

Developing Sports
for Winter Paralympics

New sports are also being considered for the Winter Paralympics. Thor Kleppe, ice sports chairman of the IPC Sports Council Executive Committee, shares his recollections on his efforts to win acceptance for wheelchair dancing, ice sledge hockey, and ice sledge racing.

"I started with the disabled sports in 1972, and my first Olympics was in Toronto, and then I spent seven years as a coach for the national swimming team in Norway. I was very much interested in winter sports, and I was educated as a teacher of sports in the university in Stockholm, Sweden. That was where I met my wife, who was a wheelchair user, and we started with wheelchair dance. In the beginning it was only done in Sweden, and I thought that it might be a good thing to do because it has something to do with integrating the able-bodied and disabled people.

"So we started to spread it, and we started an international competition. Now about 25 or 26 countries have the wheelchair dance competition. I know that many nations look at dance as an art and not as a sport, but here in Scandinavia and in Europe it is very hard training in ordinary dance and also in wheelchair dance. We don't look at it as an art, but I know that people from 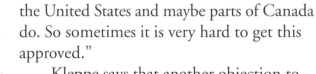 the United States and maybe parts of Canada do. So sometimes it is very hard to get this approved."

Kleppe says that another objection to wheelchair dance is that one of the competitors is able-bodied, and some members of IPC believe that Paralympic sports must be limited to the athlete with a disability.

Japan and Korea, as well as several European countries, took part in an international competition in Oslo in November 1996. Plans are under way to arrange a Wheelchair Dance World Championship in 1997.

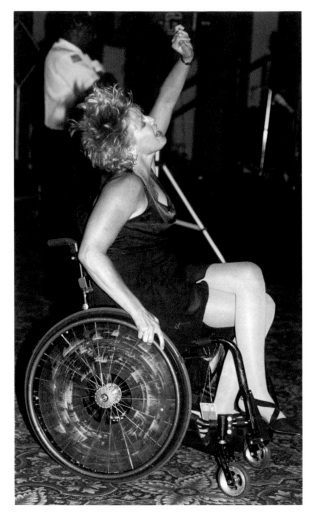

Kleppe says that if ballroom dancing becomes part of the Olympics, that should help the status of the sport, as does the fact that they are now a member of ISOD. In addition, wheelchair dance has many advantages in a country where weather severely limits athletic participation. Wheelchair dance is of course done indoors, and when done properly is good training for other sports, Kleppe says. It is an especially good sport for those in early stages of rehabilitation.

"That's where we started in the beginning. We have a centre outside of Oslo centre for paraplegics and tetrapalegics and amputees, and that is where we also started to show this sport and talk about it. There was great interest in it because they can do this after they are finished with training and practice with the physiotherapist. They could meet after supper, and listen to music and move along with some of the nurses and some of the physiotherapists. So that is how it started. They liked it very much."

He sees another advantage. "What I discovered when I started with my wife in 1977 was that people who watched us didn't see the wheelchair. They just saw a couple dancing on the floor, and we could do cha cha cha, and rumba and jive like normal people."

Thor Kleppe has also been involved with ice sports. He started with ice sledge racing, which is similar to speed skating. Then he got involved in sledge hockey, which was already being played in Sweden. He recalls, "I said that this was something that must be good for disabled persons, because first of all, we don't have many sports that we can do in the wintertime, and besides, it's a team sport and it is always fun to do a team sport." Competition with Canada followed. The first International Paralympic Championships were held in

Lillehammer with five nations competing. Kleppe believes there soon will be 10 or 12 countries competing in this sport, with Japan training fiercely for Nagano.

He says, "We are also planning another project now, because you have ice hockey rinks in almost every country in the world. We have gotten questions from Arabic people who want me to introduce sledge hockey down there because they have two indoor rinks. I thought that maybe as an extra sport we could introduce the short track that they have for everybody in the ice hockey rink, and I think that this is something that we would like to show in Nagano. We would only have to angle two blades a little bit, and then we could introduce a short rink for disabled people."

SECTION III: *Events & Technology*

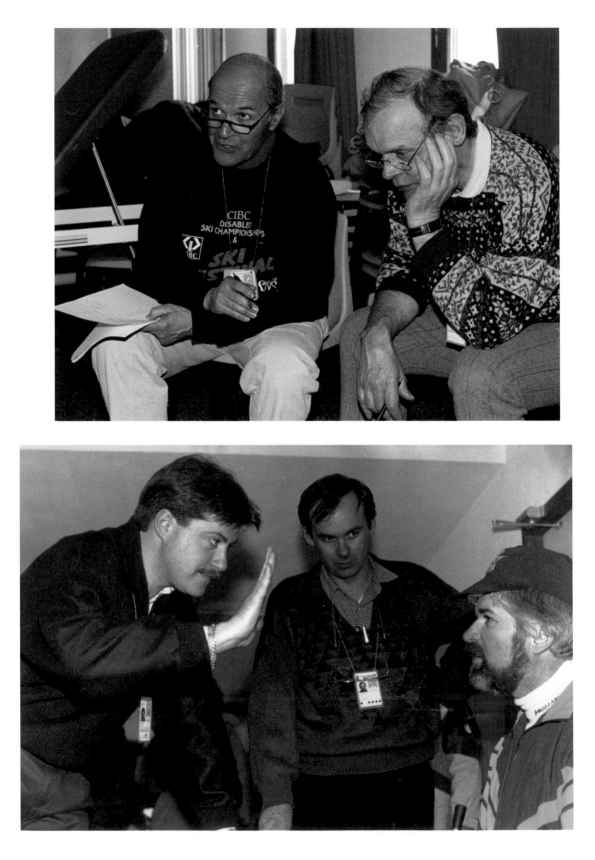

Events and Classification

SUMMER EVENTS

Archery
Athletics
Boccia
Cycling
Equestrian
Fencing
Football
Goalball
Judo
Powerlifting
Rugby
Shooting
Swimming
Table Tennis
Tennis
Volleyball
  • sitting,
  • standing
Wheelchair Basketball
Yachting

WINTER EVENTS

Alpine skiing
Biathlon
Ice sledge racing
Nordic cross-country
   skiing
Sledge hockey

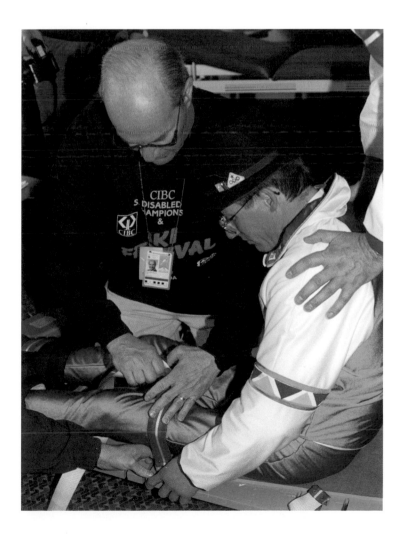

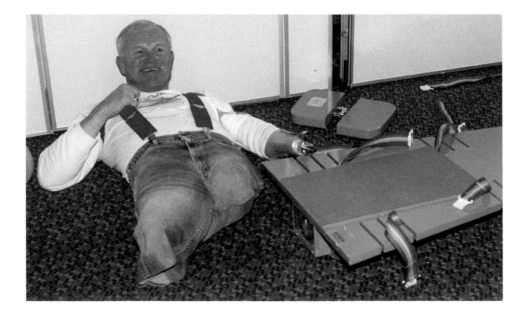

Classification of Athletes

In order to provide a level playing field where athletes can compete fairly with their peers, each Paralympic athlete is classified according to disability. This is of course done in able-bodied sport as well: a middleweight boxer is not put in the ring with a heavyweight boxer.

In the past these divisions were based solely on medical classification: spinal cord injury athletes did not compete against amputee athletes, for example. The next method was functional classification: all athletes in the same class have similar levels of function in such areas as range of motion, co-ordination and balance. Given the fact that Paralympians include athletes with cerebral palsy, blindness, spinal cord injury or disease, and dwarfism, as well as les autres and those who are amputees, comparing levels of function can be very complicated.

Presently classification is moving towards functional classification by sport. The classifier observes the athlete performing the sport; all athletes with similar capability to actually do the sport would be in the same class. Mirre Kipfer, IPC Alpine Committee member and classifier, explains. "In basketball you test what the person in a wheelchair can do with a ball, the movements that they do in basketball. In Nordic skiing you test them neurologically, but then also on a track: they have to go uphill and downhill so that you can really see what they are able to do."

Classifiers face two main problems, Kipfer explains. "Sometimes athletes try to cheat, to hide what they can really do. They are athletes who want to be in a class

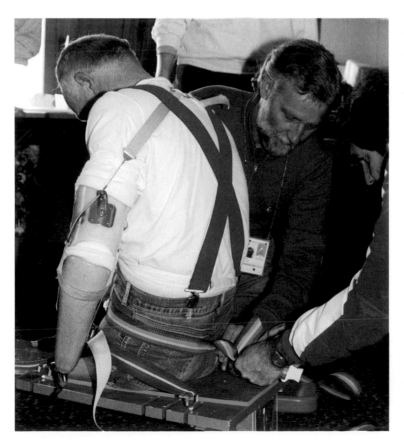

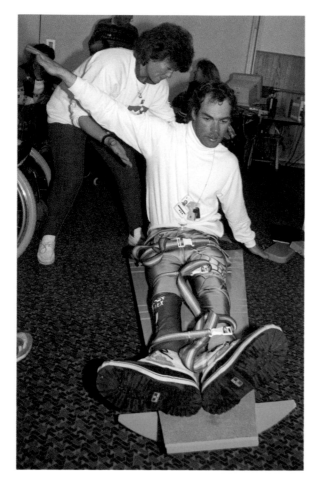

that is more advantageous for them. In testing and classification they don't show what they really can do. They try to show that they are not able to do some movement, and that is why we have started functional testing.

"The second problem is that when you have a very good athlete who is very well trained in the sport, you don't want to punish that person for their good performance. He or she might be an elite athlete doing a very good sport performance, and you might be tempted to say "OK, he is doing so well he must be in another class."

"We do try to get fewer classes so that we don't get, for example, 10 or 12 gold medals in alpine sports. We try to review the classes, but you always have borderline cases and it is always difficult. In winter the aim is to have three classes, like sitting, standing and blind: that is certainly the future that we are all looking to. For that we still have a long way to go."

With all the advances in training and equipment, Paralympic athletes are also making rapid advances. Some say that the Paralympics should include only those elite athletes who function at the highest athletic level. Others say it is time to eliminate some of the "less-disabled" athletes, since they could in many cases compete against able-bodied athletes.

Jens Bromann, IPC first vice president, comments on this. "It depends on what sport we are speaking about. Even though I have been involved in blind sports for many years, I am very open to discuss how many classes blind people should be divided into, because I find in some sports you do not even have to distinguish between blind and partially sighted.

"In some sports you could have just one class, and in other sports it is maybe necessary to have two or three classes. In some sports you should not be regarded as being disabled if you are classified B3, which means that you have vision up to l/10.

"You can as a disabled person compete with the able-bodied today, but the question is if sports for the disabled should include B3 athletes in their sports. I think they should in many sports, but maybe not in all sports."

Carol Mushett, technical director of Cerebral Palsy International Sports and Recreation Association (CP-ISRA) and a professor teaching rehabilitation at Georgia State University, discusses the difficulty in grouping athletes with cerebral palsy with athletes of other disability groups. "Cerebral palsy is not really one condition; it is a group of conditions that vary greatly and are dynamic or fluctuating versus static. Little research has been done with regard to the validity of combining individuals who

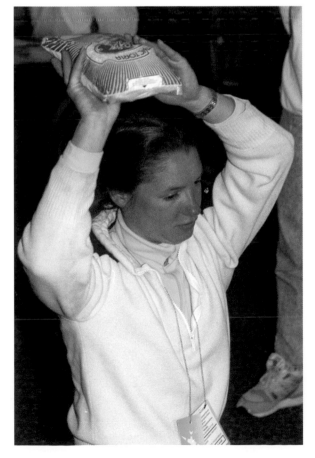

have a fluctuating disability with individuals who have a static disability. A disability like an amputation, for example, doesn't change. The degree of impairment is the same at the beginning, the middle, and the end of the race. However, with cerebral palsy the degree of spasticity could vary tremendously over the course of the race. So what you are trying to do with classification is to quantify the amount of impairment that a person has, and then equate that with something else. With cerebral palsy, it's like a moving picture, and which frame of the moving picture do you qualify in order to place that person against someone whose disability doesn't change? What we need is to develop some scientific principles to determine which disabilities are equivalent if we are going to combine them."

Elizabeth Dendy, president of CP-ISRA, is concerned about how the elite athlete is defined. She says, "I think we have really got to redefine our concept of what excellence in sport is. We look at it from the able-bodied frame of mind. Nobody who has seen boccia played at a high level doubts the amount of skill that those athletes show despite their severe disabilities, or doubts the amount of training they put in, the way they use the release of spasms and the timing of that in order to achieve the incredible skill that they get.

"We have got to re-educate people that that is skill, and that severely disabled people can be top athletes. I am very distressed to think that, in having full-medal events in the Olympics, we perpetuate the picture that the wheelchair paraplegic athlete is what we mean by the disabled athlete. We do ill service to the rest of the disabled sport world by perpetuating that end. We have to educate the general public and the world of mainstream sport that athletes who lack the chief characteristics of excellence in sport—balance, co-ordination and fluency, what we like to think of as nice-looking movement—that athletes can lack those qualities and still have real skill if we understand the nature of the sport.

"We all recognise that having 60 gold medals in one swimming event as we had in Seoul is ridiculous, and is not accepted as top sport, so we have to find ways of cutting back the number of classes so that we can show that a top disabled swimmer in a 100 metre event is the top. CP-ISRA is doing every-

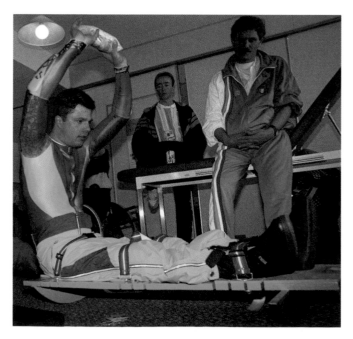

thing it possibly can to try and develop and assist the process of integrating all our disability groups into a functional class. But it mitigates severely those with CP.

"You have only got to watch two wheelchair people at a starting line of 100 metres; the paraplegic would be 50 yards along before the CP could even start on some occasions. So in principle we want to do it. But we have to safeguard the interests of our athletes, and this is particularly true in many track and field events. We have achieved it in table tennis. We have now achieved it in lawn bowling. Some of our swimmers can compete as well, but in some track and field events we are very concerned that IPC recognise the need for special chances for those with CP.

"It is not only CP people who lose out on this. Some of your severe quads with spinal cord injuries and severe les autres can also be penalised in a straight functional classification. But we do feel passionately that they must be given an equal chance, because they do have in most cases a very great disadvantage against other athletes.

"I think that we have got over the prejudices that we had against us. Nobody actually wanted us at the games when we first came in. This was way back in the early days. But we have got over that in many cases because the athletes themselves have shown what good competitors and what wonderful people they are, and the prejudice is now being suffered by those with learning disabilities. I do hope that people get over that prejudice as well."

Hans Lindström says, "The sports world for disabled and able bodied alike mainly include non-Olympic or non-Paralympic competition programs. Every sport cannot and should not be Olympic or Paralympic. That is reserved for the sports with the greatest spread in the world, those which draw the most athletes into their ranks, and which therefore are interesting to watch for a broader public. The Olympic and Paralympic Games are the quadrennial showcases of the cream of world sports."

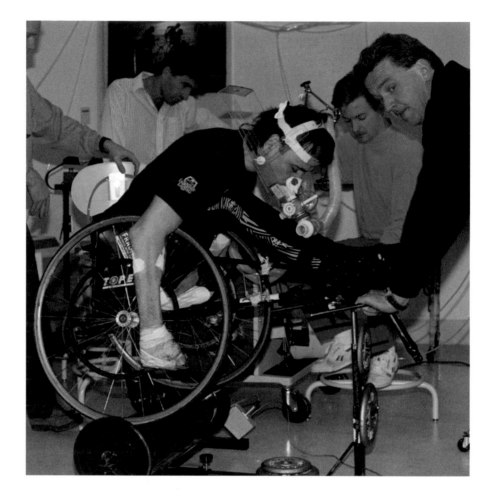

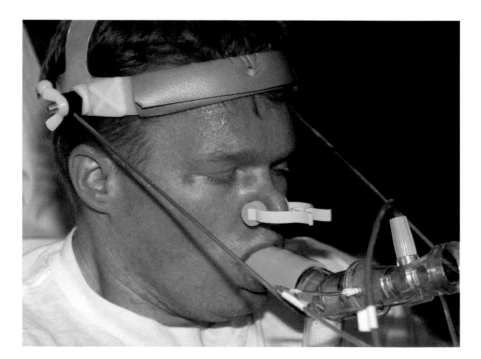

Performance

The technology of disabled sport changes rapidly. Often less-advantaged athletes suffer as a result. Sometimes it is the equipment, not the athlete, that fails.

Jeff Adams, wheelchair racer, says, "The technology we're using is probably only being used by five percent of the world. I remember in Korea watching the Mexicans race in chairs that were just garbage; they'd made them at home and they were piece-meal equipment, but they were fighting it out in the semi-finals and every once in a while one of them would make it into a final. I don't remember them medalling, but I remember thinking that, man, if these guys ever get good chairs—look at what they're doing with the garbage they're in. Sure enough, there were two in the finals at Olympics in '92 because they'd got good equipment, and two in finals in Atlanta, and Mendoza won the 5k; the Mexicans all of a sudden are a power because they got the equipment."

Pat Griffin, basketball player, has seen tremendous changes in his equipment over the years. He says, "When I first started playing in

1978, I had a old E & J hospital chair, hard rubber wheels, wear on the tires, armrests on it, a back going up to my shoulders, and handlebars back there which basically prevented you from leaning back and getting your upper body into moving your chair. So I guess the modification I did on my first chair was first rip those armrests off. You take the brakes off the chair, because you don't need brakes; you just stop with your hands.

"Then people started showing up with bicycle tires with air in them, which allowed you to go faster. The next big thing was the development of a truly light sport chair. The hospital chairs we were using were 35-50 pounds; the new lightweight sport chairs are about 25 pounds. That made a tremendous difference. Then engineering came in, and I think the next big development was people started putting camber on their back wheels, and this allowed you to turn a lot quicker, rather than having just straight up-and-down wheels. You may

have compromised an inch or a half inch in your height because when you put the camber on it, it lowers you a little bit, but it gives you a wider wheel base, and your stability is much improved. The chairs are now 12 to 15 pounds, so you are taking five pounds off a 20-pound chair, which is 20% of the weight; that makes quite a bit of difference. The next major thing to come was the three-wheeled chair, and once again that improved your maneuverability because you only had one caster touching the court rather than two for less friction.

"Now everyone is into strapping. You strap yourself in so that your chair moves with any movement that your body makes. So those have been the changes in a quick synopsis over the period of years."

While improved equipment is an effective way to improve performance, some athletes find other ways to get an advantage over their competition. Dr. Michael Riding, IPC medical officer, says, "In any elite sport some athletes are going to try to seek an edge any way they can, and that includes dope taking. Dope taking is treated with the same gravity by the International Paralympic Committee as it is by the International Olympic Committee. We use their rules, as modified for athletes with disabilities, and we also use the same list of banned substances as the IOC. One modification that we have made is our Medication Advisory Panel process, which enables an athlete who is taking a drug that is on the banned list to have the chance at competing, provided that we on the panel think that it is not going to give him or her an unfair advantage."

SECTION IV: *Profiles*

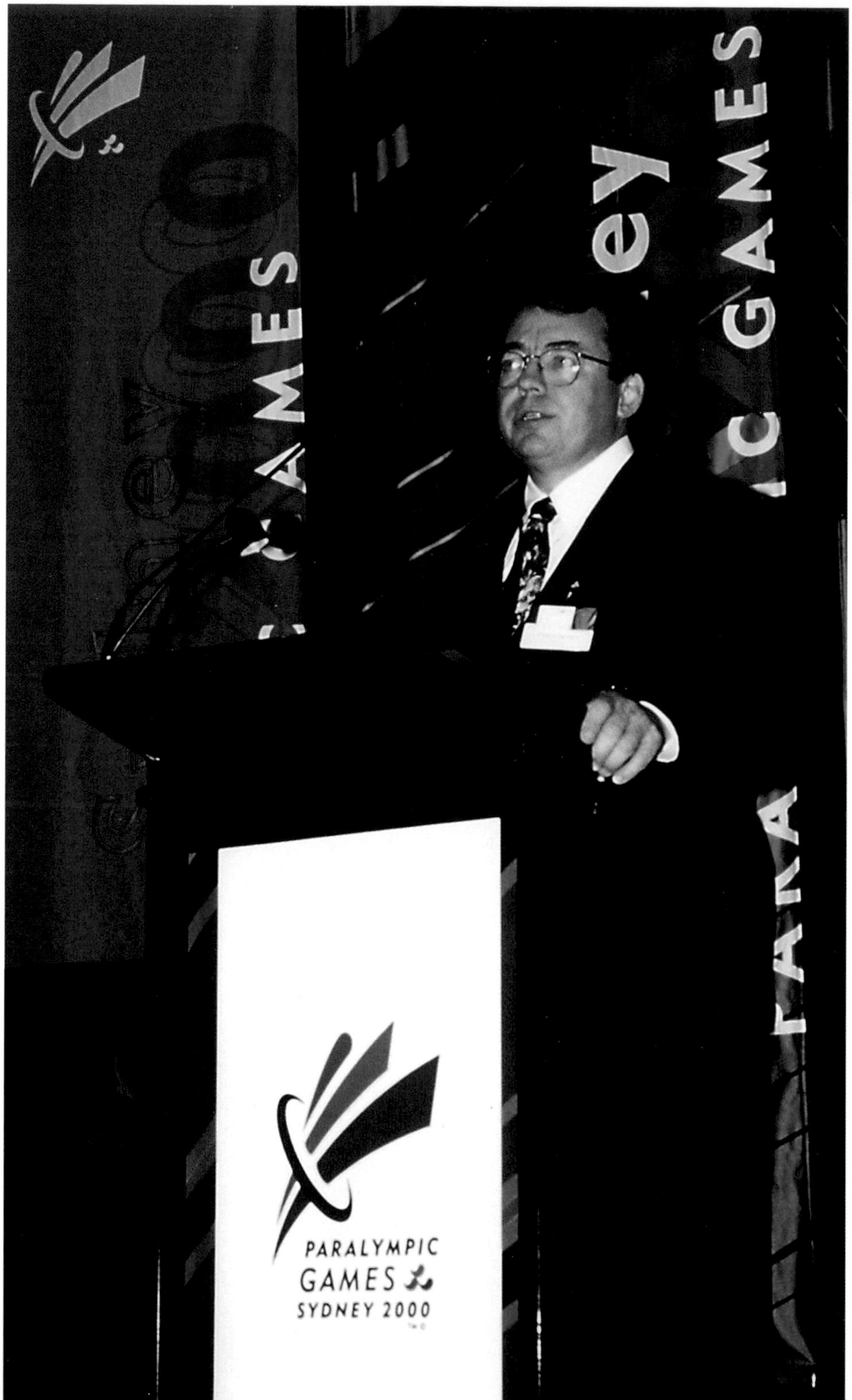
PARALYMPIC
GAMES
SYDNEY 2000

Dr. Robert Steadward:
Canada

"The success of IPC is very much the work of the president. The history of the movement will give Bob Steadward the title of Father of the Modern Paralympics."

*Bernard Atha,
INAS-FMH
Former President*

Not only is Dr. Robert Steadward the first (and only) president of the International Paralympic Committee to date, he has three other full-time jobs. He is a professor in the Faculty of Physical Education and Recreation at the University of Alberta, director of the Rick Hansen Centre, and director of the Edmonton Sport Medicine Institute. He has won innumerable awards for his contributions to disablity sport and is a world-class scholar and researcher.

Bob Steadward keeps a schedule that would kill most men. He travels incessantly, using weekends and holidays to take care of Paralympic business around the world. His dedication to his work is exceeded only by his commitment to his family: his wife, Laura, and their daughters, Tommi Lynn and Bobbi Jo. Time at home is a precious commodity to Steadward, who has always managed to make his daughter's important field hockey games or dance recitals. His family does worry about the time Steadward spends in the air, and the occasional earthquake and bomb threat he's met in his travels, but has developed its own routine in Steadward's absence.

These days Steadward is a veteran traveller who has mastered the problems of jet lag and lost luggage. He learned these lessons the hard way, however; one trip to Oslo barely escaped disaster. He recalls, "I knew I had lots of time. Everything was perfect as I flew into Calgary. Maybe too perfect."

The rest of the trip included an engine fire, circling to burn off fuel, missed connections, lost luggage, and an early morning trip to a friend's clothing store to buy clothes to wear to his meeting. These days Steadward boards his plane dressed in a suit and carrying his luggage, ready for anything.

Born in Eston, a small town in Saskatchewan, Canada, Bob Steadward grew up with sport as part of his life. He remembers being given his first pair of skates when he was four years old, and spending hours playing hockey on a nearby frozen river. Another influential part of his childhood was his grandmother. After suffering a stroke that paralysed her right side, Marion Steadward lived with Bob's family on and off for nine years.

In high school Steadward lettered in six different sports over three years, and in 1964 he enrolled at the University of Alberta in Edmonton. One of his courses required he do a practicum, so he volunteered to coach the Edmonton Handicaddies, a wheelchair basketball club. Dr. Steadward's achievements in the world of adapted sport began with this experience. He says, "I never looked differently at people, whether they were in wheelchairs or walking. I didn't know about visual impairment, cerebral palsy, spinal cord injury, or amputation. All I knew was that these people played a sport called wheelchair basketball.

"The more I got to know them, the more I learned about disabilities: their nature, their severity, their etiology and causes. This became part of my academic career as well. What made these people special was how they were able to deal with their disabilities and go on with living. They never thought that their disabilities would in any way limit their ability to participate in anything they wanted to do."

Steadward's friend Dr. Bob Jackson was president of the Canadian Wheelchair Sports Association. The success Steadward made of coaching the Handicaddies, and the influence of his friend, made it a logical next step for Steadward to accept more responsibility. He

helped organize the first wheelchair sport national championships in Canada, which were held in Edmonton in 1968.

Steadward soon met his first challenge as an administrator: a postal strike. He needed a way to communicate with various provinces and clubs about the games. That's when he met the man who became his closest and life-long friend, Gary McPherson.

McPherson lived in the University Hospital in Ward 67, the polio ward. He was a ham-radio operator. Every Sunday morning at 9:30 Steadward met McPherson and his roommates, where they connected with other hams in major centres across Canada. Through this linkage Steadward and others were able to organize the games.

Later Steadward coached the swim, track and wheelchair basketball teams of the first wheelchair club that started in Edmonton, the Paralympic Sports Association.

Reg McClellan, veteran wheelchair basketball player, recalls, "One of the things that Bob instilled in a team was that it wasn't that you put your five best players out there and you beat the other team, but rather each time out was an opportunity to strengthen your squad. Bob made sure that the weak links were as strong as they could possibly be so that as a unit the team was able to do the best possible job when it counted."

The only way the disabled sport movement could receive provincial government funding was through a provincial association. None existed, so in 1970-71 Steadward created the Alberta Wheelchair Sports Association. He served as founder-president and took teams to national championships.

In 1971 Steadward headed the Canadian delegation to the Pan-American Games in Jamaica. He was required to be incredibly flexible; some athletes participated in as many as eight events.

Next Steadward coached the Canadian National Team at the 1972 Paralympic Games in Heidelberg, Germany, and the 1973 International Stoke Mandeville Games in Aylesbury. Here Steadward first met Sir Ludwig Guttmann. Steadward took teams to Stoke Mandeville every year (except Paralympic years) until 1980.

In 1976 Steadward was responsible for Canadian team operations at the Torontolympiad, and in the 1980's was president of the Canadian Federation of Sport Organizations for the Disabled (CFSOD).

1977-8 had brought a different sort of challenge: the creation of the University of Alberta's Research and Training Centre for the Physically Disabled, later renamed the Rick Hansen Centre. Steadward recalls, "I was concerned that our disabled athletes did not have a training centre, or access to sports scientists to do assessments and evaluations and design training programs. So in the fall of 1978, I opened up a centre at the University. It changed from being an athletes' centre to more of a general health, fitness and lifestyle centre that would cater to the needs of all people with a disability interested in fitness and in becoming more integrated into society at large. Not only do we provide the environment and de-sign a lot of training programs, we also have a worldwide reputation because of the kinds of research and leadership that we provide in adapted sport and adapted physical activity. A day doesn't go by when I don't get a request from somewhere in the world wanting access to our centre, or asking us to come over to another country to set up a similar program."

It was at the 1980 Arnhem Games that Steadward again encountered the problems involved in four different organizations running one competition. Because of CFSOD, on the Canadian team there was no distinction made between the blind competitor or the competitor in a wheelchair. As a result Steadward found the team easy to administer; it was likely the most successful, sophisti-cated team ever. But he was frustrated by the problems of dealing with all the different international organizations for sports at the Arnhem Games. He had to consult not only with the organizing committee, but in dealing with swimming, depending on the kind of a competitor, he'd have to deal with a technical officer from three different international disability-specific organizations. There were other natural changes taking place, too, such as disabled athletes be-

ing accepted as skilled athletes at able-bodied swim clubs. It was time to find a way to bring athletes together.

Steadward's view of the need for an international umbrella organization for disabled sport was shared by many people around the world. Soon after the Arnhem Games the Interna-tional Coordinating Committee was formed.

In 1983-84, with Anne Merklinger and other members of CFSOD, Steadward was involved in the development of a ma-jor proposal to look at a new structure for disablity sport which would have democratic national representation designed on a sport model, rather than a medical or rehabilitation model. This proposal created much discussion around the world.

Now, because of the proposal created by Steadward and CFSOD, the IOC's call for a single organization to negotiate on behalf of disabled sport, and because of the pressure of the various nations, what was probably the most significant histori-cal event ever in disability sport took place in 1987. At the Arnhem Seminar an agreement was reached to create a new worldwide democratic organization based on membership of nations.

Steadward was instrumental in the development of this change in direction. As a direct result of using his diplomatic skills to share his views of how the organization should look, in 1989 he was elected as the inaugral president of the International Paralympic Committee.

During the transition period that followed, various countries were bidding on the 2000 Olympic and Paralympic Games. Steadward dis-

covered that his new position was not without its challenges. He travelled to Berlin, where, he says, "The bid to host the Olympic and Paralympic Games in Berlin was not totally acceptable to a group of dissidents who really wanted to create problems for anyone associated with the bids. Any time I went to Berlin, I always had bodyguards because threats had come from these various groups.

"We were staying in the former east side of Berlin close to a park near the Brandenberg Gate. I told the security people I would like to go there each morning for a run, and one of the bodyguards who was a runner met me the next morning. He was carrying his gun and his walkie-talkie in case we got into trouble, and off we went.

"Five kilometres later he was huffing and puffing, and I was just getting warmed up, and was leaving him behind. I slowed down to run with him, but he was absolutely exhausted when we got back to the hotel.

"The next day was different; he ran with me part way, and then someone else ran with me the next leg, then someone else ran the next leg, and when I was on the streets they would both be in the car, and they would drive alongside of me so that they didn't have to run.

China also bid on the 2000 Games, and it was in Beijing where Steadward was most taken aback by his VIP treatment. "Being a close friend of Deng Pufang, I have always been treated very well; when I arrive at the airport I don't go through the normal procedures of customs and immigration. On one particular occasion, they met me at the airport and put my limousine into a

motorcade to go to the hotel. I didn't know why we really needed the escort; we were driving down the middle of a brand-new highway leading from the airport to Tiananmen Square. They had closed the highway off, and all the traffic was lined up for miles off all these exit ramps. I felt pretty special, but it was also quite embarrassing.

"When I got to the hotel, I wanted to make sure that I could get my runs in, but it was very difficult. I could never shake the media.

"So I said I'd fix them. I got up one morning about 5 o'clock and went out for my run. I usually ran from the hotel down to Tiananmen Square and back. It was only about a 10-kilometre loop, but it was a pleasant run; you got to see the local people in Beijing getting ready to go to the market, and I enjoyed it very much.

"No sooner had I started to run down the street when this little red car came buzzing out between two buildings. Six people were jammed into it, one guy driving, a couple guys in the back seat, one guy hanging on to the back bumper with a television camera, and a couple sitting on the front fender who were also taking pictures. They followed me all the way up to Tiananmen Square and back. That night on national television there it was: me jogging up to the square and back. It's amazing what you can't get away with in those areas."

During the 1988 Winter Olympic Games in Calgary, Alberta, President Steadward had met the IOC president, Mr. Juan Antonio Samaranch, to discuss how athletes with a disability could be included in the Olympics. At the conclusion of the meeting, Mr. Samaranch invited a proposal on how events for athletes with a disability might be integrated into the Olympic Games.

In 1990, with the hope of using amateur sport as a vehicle to support and enhance the quality of life for people with a disability, the IPC approved the creation of a Presidential committee on integration: the Commission for Inclusion of Athletes with a Disability (CIAD). One of its six goals was to help get selective full medal events for athletes with a disability into major international competitions.

President Steadward's presentation to the IOC Joint Assembly on December 17, 1994, was the first ever on disability sport. In his address Steadward said, "The goal of the Olympic movement is to contribute to building a peaceful and better world by educating youth through sport practised without discrimination of any kind. Discrimination, therefore, was not acceptable in either spirit or in practice on the basis of disability. Discrimination on the basis of disability was no different and was as objectionable as discrimination on the basis of race, colour, sex, religion or politics."

From 1989 to the present the IPC has had tremendous success under President Steadward's leadership. While growing from 37 to 150 nations, the organization has created a sport-organization constitution, a marketing committee, a media commission, a medical committee, and a technical department. Hans Lindström says, "I have known every person in the top echelons of the sports world for the disabled in different times of its development. There is no one who could have done a better job than Bob has done in getting the IPC ship under way and accelerating."

Jens Bromann says of Dr. Steadward, "He has given sports for the disabled and our organization a direction, not only for the first decade, but into the twenty-first century."

Barbara Campbell, Steadward's executive assistant, says of his success, "I think Dr. Steadward's magic is hope. Who doesn't want to be involved in a future that has hope in it?"

Gary McPherson describes Dr. Steadward's impact this way:

"Bob Steadward is like someone in the banking business who starts out as a teller, works his way up to manager, and finally becomes

CEO of the largest bank in Canada, learning every aspect of the business. Bob's done everything from sweeping floors, to coaching, to organizing, administrating, to leading, being a visionary, educating, tutoring, consoling and cajoling. He understands every facet of sport with disabilities, including the research, because he's done it all. There is nobody else on earth who has that kind of collective insight."

Jeff Adams:
Canada

"I truly believe the valiant struggle to succeed is such an important thing: not just the winning, but the overcoming of obstacles, which everybody does, disabled or not."

Jeff Adams trains full time and competes in as many as 20 competitions a year. He says, "I think of what I do as a performance. If you cross the line first, you celebrate, and you make the crowd part of your celebration lap. Just the pure show of athleticism is so neat to be able to do."

Jeff has held two world and four Canadian records. He's also had the opportunity to deal with Olympic disappointment. He recalls, "I was really in good shape going into the Barcelona Olympics, but with 300 metres left to go in my 1500m race, the push ring on my right rear wheel fell off."

Another disappointment occurred at the 1996 Olympics in Atlanta. Jeff broke the world record six weeks before trials for the Olympics and was undefeated for 18 months in the 1500m. Then he got the flu, and didn't make it past the semi-final.

"I've been dreaming about the Olympic demonstration event for 12 years now, and it seems like every time something happens. It's tough to go back to the Paralympics racing against the same guys who compete in the Olympics because then you think of what could have been. In Barcelona I won a silver medal in the 800 metres and beat a bunch of guys who were in the demonstration event; I came back to Atlanta and won the 800 metres. But the disappointment is something that will make me a better athlete and a better person, so I have to take comfort in that."

Jeff's competitive attitude is equalled by his physical endurance. He says, "I win a lot of races just by toughing it out. I get a lot of that attitude from my father. When I was a kid, I was convinced that he picked up the back end of the Volkswagen with one hand, and fixed the transmission with the other. He's always shown me in a very quiet, back seat sort of way that's it's good to be tough; it's good to be able to put your shoulder into it and get it done."

Jeff's mental toughness helped his performance in the Commonwealth Games in Victoria, Canada, in 1994. A comment was made that disabled athletes had no business being included in these games. Jeff says, "The best way to get through to people like that is not to talk to them, because you can't change their minds that way, but to show them."

He went into the semi-final and pushed as hard as he could to show how fast wheelchair racers could go in the 800 metres. Normally Jeff can hear other racers coming up on him, but not in that race. He recalls, "It wasn't a token round of applause that we got; it was people standing up and stomping and screaming and slapping each other on the back."

"In terms of performance, the games are a showcase to display athletic ability, and if the crowd appreciates your performance, what else is there to talk about?"

The organisers agreed: faced with having to refund tickets because some of the preliminaries had been cancelled, they asked the wheelchair racers to do a demonstration 1500 metres.

"That's one of the things I'm most proud of; we were able to put on a show at one of the biggest able-bodied sporting events in the world. There was no tokenism in that at all; people get real honest when they're talking about money."

Jeff loves to talk to children about his sport. "Kids are excited by the technology and the speed: when they see a racing chair made out of aluminium carbon fibre, and I can lift it over my head with one hand, and I tell them I can go 90k an hour down a hill, you see their faces light up.

"Disabled kids who have lived their whole lives trying to get around their physical disability see someone like them making his living through physical activity. This possibility never occurred to a lot of them. So whether or not they want to go on and try to do something physical, they at least see the potential for choice."

Chantal Benoit:
Canada

"Be in love with what you do, and do it the best that you can."

Known by many as the Michael Jordan of women's basketball, Chantal Benoit's offensive skills dominate play so effectively that an opposing team developed the "Chantal defence" to try to stop her. It didn't work. Chantal, or "Neuf," is a member of the Canadian team who won gold in Barcelona in 1992. They outplayed the highly favoured Americans, with Chantal scoring 18 points in the 35-26 victory. The Canadians won gold again in 1996.

"Playing on that team in Atlanta was great. We were really centred on our game. For each move of the opposite team, we adjusted our game, defence or offence, so it was very hard for the other teams to read what we were doing."

A former competitive diver, Chantal has competed in wheelchair basketball at four Paralympic Games and two world championships. With gold at Barcelona her goal, she moved to Ottawa to train, leaving behind family and friends. She recalls, "I learned more in one year than I did eight years in my region. At the same time I started to learn English and decided to go back to school after seven or eight years."

Chantal completed her degree in sociology, and has a new career in web-page design. She says, "It is something that I really enjoy and I will do my best to bring my knowledge as high as possible, to keep on learning."

She brings this same attitude to all she does, including her training program. She says, "I can relate to the social life that you don't have when you do a sport. But I am in love with what I am doing, so it's not called sacrifice for me."

But like most Paralympians, Chantal and her team-mates do make sacrifices. "Since 1990 when we started to win with our first bronze medal at the first world championship for women, our team became a big family. To play the best that you can as a team you have to play together. Because the financial help or aid is not there, a lot of women on the team took the initiative together." They trained in several cities to get ready for Atlanta, team members in each place opening their homes to their team-mates.

Chantal describes the result. "In amateur basketball everyone has a position and a role to do, and with that team, we were not the starting five; we were the starting 12. Everybody was able to replace everybody, because we knew each other better than ever. We were there to play together and have fun."

Chantal has a great passion for her game. "I like the intensity, the speed, the aggressiveness, and all that you can do physically and technically. I am in a period right now of my basketball career where I am looking for knowledge in offence and defence strategy. But it's so good to try to work with five people to defeat any defence in front of you or to play the best defence against any other team as a five and as a unit. I just give my heart and play with my heart."

One of her favourite memories of Atlanta is having a special photograph taken. "We were the gold winners at the Atlanta Games. Everybody was excited. And I was excited. That feeling stayed with me for so long a time. One day before leaving the Olympic Village in Atlanta, Bob Peterson, the photographer, came to me and asked me if I would be part of a picture. I've known him for a long time; he always gave his heart to the Canadian team. For me it was an experience to be part of the project made by Robert.

"I had a big Canadian flag around my neck and I had to roll down the hill holding the flag to make a wind effect. I had to go up that hill about 25 times. A gentleman who was a security guard or a policeman

really gave his time to help fix the flag every time I went up the hill. That was really enjoyable!"

Chantal's joy and passion for life come through in all she does. "When I do presentations, the basic message I try to give to people is that co-operation and collaboration will make a population come together. If you want to go somewhere, you have to have co-operation between each other and make the emphasis on the positive things."

Matthias Berg:
Germany

"I was always interested in what was possible for me, not to be better than the others, but to meet my own potential for my mind and my body."

Concert musician, Winter and Summer Paralympian, administrator, Matthias Berg has been a dedicated performer for much of his life. Competing from 1980 to 1994 in both skiing and athletics, and touring the world playing the French horn, Berg credits sport and music for shaping him into the person he is today. He has won 14 gold, nine silver, and six bronze medals in the World Championships and Paralympics, Winter and Summer, and 39 German championships in athletics and alpine skiing.

Berg says, "I always loved sport, and of course it helped a lot to get the acceptance of other people, and made it easier to carry on a conversation with people. Sport was a way to maybe reach my personal maximum."

Berg's entire family encouraged him to get involved in sport. He recalls, "My father had a friend whose son was disabled through thalidomide, as I was, and he asked if I would like to go to a ski camp just for fun, and for a skiing course. I did that when I was about 13 or 14. Through that group of people, I got into athletics also, and competed in very small sports competitions." By the age of 19, Berg's skills had developed to the point where he competed in his first Paralympics in 1980: Winter Games in Oslo, Summer Games in Arnhem.

A graduate of Freiburg in law and music, today Berg works as a civil servant for the Ministry of Internal Affairs, and heads a department of 75 people. He says, "Everybody on the team has his role. In sport I was convinced that the training was not only for me; it was also for the trainer. The trainer and I and the team are only successful if we give the best we can."

Berg feels the team must set a goal, and then develop a plan to reach it. He says, "It is almost the same as in training. You go step by step to reach the goal, and do the best that you possibly can. That idea has affected my whole life and my profession."

Success for Berg is very much a mental exercise. He says, "It may sound a little arrogant, but in every part of my life, sport or music or my profession or whatever, I always wanted to be as good as possible. For me it is important to find my head, my brain, is in order and under control. The mental work before training, during training and after the training, as well as in competition, for me was very important. I knew that if my personal attitude before the competition was OK, I won the competition."

Two winning moments stand out in Berg's mind. He recalls, "The best moment I ever had in athletics in the Paralympics was in the big Olympic Stadium in Seoul, where there were 50 or 60,000 people shouting during the 200 metre race I competed in. It was . . . wow. It got directly under my skin. It was unbelievably impressive."

Another winning moment was in 1990 at the World Championships in Colorado. Berg won his first gold medal in an international race in the Super G. Berg says, "It was the best gold medal I ever had, I think, in my life, because it was much easier for me in athletics to get the gold medal, but in winter sports I had to work much harder. So that was the biggest moment I ever had."

The ceremonies of the Games are also wonderful memories. Berg says, "Walking into the stadium in the Opening Ceremonies in Seoul was a very special feeling. There are all those people who want to see the games, and who expect a lot of the competitors. You feel very comfortable, very accepted and very happy."

"One of my best feelings, I think, is the Closing Ceremonies. They always have a little bit of the laughing and the crying eye, because everything is over. Always they have a lot of tension, and a lot of excitement also. Everybody there is interested, and they like the sport and the people. Every time it is unique."

Ann Cody:
United States

By the time Ann Cody was sixteen she competed in every season in every sport available to her. Her family was very supportive of her hopes to go on to play collegiate sports. Then a viral infection damaged her spinal cord.

Cody recalls, "When I became paralyzed, it was devastating, particularly because of my goals as an athlete. My family played an integral part in my adjustment, and my high school coach was very supportive. She began researching right away to find out what kind of sport options I had available to me, because my rehabilitation hadn't included that."

Because Cody wanted to graduate on time, she went back to high school as soon as she was released from rehab. Her coach introduced her to some of the sports she had read about, including road racing, archery, basketball, and swimming. But Cody was sure she would never compete athletically again.

She recalls, "At sixteen I knew pretty clearly what my short term goals were — go to college, get a degree, and have a career. I didn't know where or even if sports fit into that."

Cody began looking for a university to attend. Her criteria were not academic standards, but which schools had ramps and accessible dorms. After much research she visited the University of Illinois. She was amazed by the accessibility of the campus, and the excellent sports program available to her.

Cody feels now that she did not give herself enough time to grieve after her illness. She recalls, "A lot of times I felt that it wasn't okay for me to feel sad, to be upset, to be hurting. I felt that I had to put on this mask so that everybody around me would be okay with who I was and the fact that I had a disability."

She used those experiences in her job in therapeutic recreation, where she worked with newly injured people on sports and fitness-related goals. Cody says, "It is important to deal for them to deal with the emotions that they are experiencing, whether it is anger or sadness, or whatever. Later there is a point in the rehabilitation process when they turn to a recreation therapist and say, I know that I am going to be able to get out of bed, shower, get dressed, maybe drive my car, semi-independently or independently, now I am ready to learn what options I have for my life. The process is different for everybody. Some people leave rehabilitation without ever getting to that point.

"That is why community-based programs such as wheelchair sports, quad rugby, and track teams are so important. Sometimes in rehabilitation the only thing that you can give people is the knowledge that those sports are out there."

Cody participated as an athlete in three Paralympics. In 1984 she played on the US Women's Basketball team at Stoke Mandeville. She loved the camaraderie of the team event, although the atmosphere was tense. She recalls, "Coming from the University of Illinois, which was where the 1984 games were supposed to be held, was the heaviest part of the experience. The British felt that the Americans let the whole world down. As a young athlete it was hard for me to experience the fact that we didn't successfully host those games."

As a child Cody dreamed of Olympic competition. That dream came true at Seoul, where she competed in the Olympic Games in the exhibition 800 metre event. She stayed on for the Paralympic Games to compete in the 1500 metre, the 5000 metre and the 10000 metre, her stronger events. She won four silver medals in Seoul. She says, "It was important for me to see those games rise to that level of significance internationally, because when I was competing in the Olympic Games just two weeks earlier, I was very clearly an afterthought. Having that tremendous experience competing in the Paralympics renewed my belief in the Olympic movement."

In 1992 Cody won bronze and gold in Barcelona. She says, "Barcelona brought the games to another level, even higher than Seoul. None of us expected it. What most athletes tell you about Barcelona was the overwhelming attendance and support from Spanish people. We were given the same facilities and the same level of service as the Olympic athletes."

When Cody returned from Barcelona, she became a spokesperson for the Atlanta Paralympic Games. She was named to the board of directors as an athlete representative, and co-chaired the Athletes Advisory Committee. Then she was asked to work for the organizing committee. She recalls, "I had to make a decision about whether I was going to compete in 1996 or work in a professional organization. I saw a need for athletes with disabilities to take leadership in the movement. This was my opportunity to give something back."

Cody was hired by the Atlanta Paralympic Organizing Committee as sport planning manager. She found this to be a positive environment where athletes' input and recommendations were very much a part of the planning process.

Chris Cohen:
England

"Honesty and fairness are the most important qualities that anybody could have. When you can say at the end of the day that what you have done has been done as honestly and fairly as you could, and you have treated everybody as well as you could do, then you can be happy with what you have done, even though you may not necessarily have achieved what you set out to achieve."

Chris Cohen has an extensive and varied background in sport. A national competitor in triple jump, Cohen retired at age 25 and took up coaching. He coached long jumper Fiona May, who went on to win the World Championship in 1995 and a silver medal in the 1996 Olympics.

A department head and physical education teacher at the high school level in England, Cohen took up officiating and has been involved in able-bodied sport at the international level for over 15 years. He got involved in wheelchair sports in 1979, and then in other disabilities at the 1984 Paralympics at Stoke Mandeville. He was technical delegate for the European Championships in 1985, and while there was asked to become chairman of the European Committee for Wheelchair Athletics. By 1988 Cohen was the only international official familiar with all the rules of all of the disability groups. He went to Seoul to teach the officials of the 1988 Paralympics, and was technical delegate for wheelchair events.

Colleagues requested Cohen stand for chairman of athletics of the IPC. He was successful, and has held this position ever since. He was technical delegate for Barcelona and Atlanta, as well as for the World Championship in 1994 in Berlin.

Cohen feels he has been greatly influenced by his experience with athletes with a disability. He recalls his first wheelchair competition. "I found very quickly that the people I was faced with were athletes in exactly the same way as all the other athletes I have ever met. Their outlook on their sport was exactly the same, and they were people that I really wanted to be involved with."

Cohen believes that Paralympic athletes "should be treated as near to able-bodied athletes as possible, bearing in mind that there are things that they do require in order to get them on the track. When they reach the competition venue, they don't require more than anyone else requires. I think that it's a question of making the similarity to other athletes more obvious than the dissimilarity."

Asked about his leadership qualities, Cohen replies, "My parents taught me that honesty and fairness are the most important qualities that anybody could have. When I became chairman of IPC Athletics, the situation could have been quite difficult because I was regarded as coming in from the wheelchair side, and people assumed that I would therefore be biased towards wheelchair athletics. I think the thing that I have worked hardest at is to make sure that people don't regard that as being the case.

"People recognise that I really don't care what their disability is. The important thing is that they all have to fit into the same system. So I don't favour one group against another because they've all got similar if not equal problems."

Cohen recalls how the Nigerian sprinter, Ajibola Adeoye, almost lost his chance to compete in Barcelona. "He arrived two hours late for his race in the 100 metres. His 100 metre heats had already been held, and I was the only person around. He started screaming and wailing and kissing my feet and saying that he had got to be allowed to run because it would be terrible if he couldn't. What had happened was that the Spaniards had produced a copy of the timetable where the time on it was 2:30 instead of 12:30. Fortunately, we managed to get a copy of his timetable and allowed him to run a time trial, and he got put into the finals because he had by far the best of times on the final line. Then he set a new world record by about a quarter of a second."

Veteran of many international competitions, Cohen finds that each one still presents surprises. "I remember in Seoul the man in charge of the field events made this marvellous speech at a reception towards the end of the competition. He felt he had done his duty to God because he had been honoured by being the field referee in the Olympics, and by doing the same job for the Paralympics, he felt that he had carried out this marvellous task for the poor old disabled. At the time I really couldn't believe that anyone could say such a thing, that one was a honour, and one was a duty."

Scott Connery:
Canada, 1973-94

His parents recall, "Scott loved to ski. No matter what the temperature, he was always ready, whether it was just for training, or to go to a competition, he was always up for it."

Scott started skiing at age 10. He joined the ski team, took some courses, and at 15 joined the race team. He was a natural but he also worked very hard. His parents remember, "He was committed to the program, pleased with it and with the people who were in it. He made some excellent friends, friends that still keep in touch with us.

"The ski program gave Scott a lot of self-confidence. He was very fortunate that his ability took him to places like France, where he competed in the Tignes Paralympics, and he was really looking forward to his second Games in Lillehammer. There was no doubt in his mind that he was going to get gold this time."

Scott's goal was to excel in the Paralympics and do well for his country. But achievement in skiing was just one of his goals. He also kept up his studies at the University of Alberta: he wanted to be a sports psychologist. He set high standards for himself, keeping up his training and commitment year round.

Scott Connery was killed in a training accident when he was preparing for Lillehammer. All who knew him knew the joy and pride Scott had in his achievements.

Elaine Ell:
Canada

"Sport is something that's a very important part of my life; it's moulded me into what I am."

As a child Elaine Ell spent most of her life at the Calgary Children's Hospital. She was always athletically inclined and liked sports, even though in those days she didn't have much opportunity to participate.

When she moved to Edmonton she started playing wheelchair basketball, organised at that time through the occupational/physical therapy department of the University Hospital, and the Paralympic Sport Association. Later she played with the Alberta Northern Lights Wheelchair Basketball Society, ending her sport career as their program co-ordinator for five years.

Ell recalls, "Participating in wheelchair sport gave me the self-confidence to mature socially and academically, and to be a contributing citizen in the community. The confidence, overall growth, and development I gained from it proves that if you want something, and you work hard, you can achieve it."

Elaine Ell always worked hard. She overcame her fear of water to hold the Canadian record in the pentathlon for a number of years. She took part in many national and international competitions, starting with the Pan-American Games in 1969, and others in Argentina, Peru, Jamaica and Mexico City. She competed at the Paralympics in Toronto, Arnhem and Seoul, various world championships and the Stoke Mandeville Games. She says, "Many times I wore two caps, serving as an athlete and as an administrator."

Competition 25 years ago was much different. Ell recalls, "In my early years we had to do everything. I can remember being in 12 events, among them javelin, table tennis and wheelchair basketball. Sometimes you found out after you got to the Pan American Games what events you were in. Maybe you hadn't done that event before. Say someone needed a doubles partner, you filled in. Most athletes today specialise in a single area, but then if someone didn't show up, you were chosen and you did it."

Ell says, "I've done many wonderful things in my life, all of them from a wheelchair. I worked for nine years with the Edmonton Oilers hockey team as assistant public relations director; the Oilers bought my first car. I met a good friend who was up playing baseball in Edmonton, and got to play catch with the New York Yankees. I travelled world-wide. I volunteered with the 1978 Commonwealth Games and Universiade '83. I made great friends both as a participant and as a spectator. I was inducted into the Alberta Sports Hall of Fame, named Canada's top female athlete, and won the MVP award at local and national level."

Although Ell wasn't a starter a lot of the time, she played for over 20 years on national and international teams, and so, she says, "I must have done something right. Maybe it was being on the bench and giving my team-mates a lift. Achievement is different for everyone. We can't all be at the top of the ladder, but just trying hard to get there and being part of a team is so very important. Even if you don't win the medal, just the opportunity to participate in the competition, whether it's local, national or international, is wonderful."

Asked about her motivation, Ell says, "Wanting to be the best motivated me, and wanting to win and represent Canada well. I wanted to help my team-mates. I had great coaches, good people who became good friends. I always wanted to do the best job possible, whether in competition, or at work, or in my daily life."

Ell won over one hundred medals in pentathlon, swimming, and basketball. Her achievements did not come easily. She says, "Most Olympic athletes spend all their time preparing and training for their sport, while many disabled athletes eight or nine years ago (and probably many today, too) had to maintain their regular jobs while trying to get ready for competition. But I don't consider that a sacrifice because I enjoyed every minute of it. It's a matter of putting your priorities where you want them."

Ell hopes that Paralympians today understand that their achievements are built on the hard work of earlier competitors. "We've made some great steps forward, and of course the benefits are now being felt as a result of some of the things we did. I wish I could still be playing, but you can't play forever. I'm happy for those who are able to benefit from all the steps that other people have made for them."

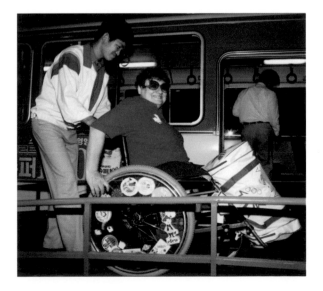

Ron Fineran:
Australia

Ron Fineran is the co-founder of the Australian Disabled Ski Federation, head of the Australian Paralympic Federation, and key member of the group that organized the bid for the 2000 Sydney Olympics and Paralympics. The polio he contracted at 19 months affected both legs and one arm, but Fineran has been an athlete since he left the polio ward at seven years of age. He recalls, "As a youngster, I was heavily involved in sport with my brother and sister and through schooling as well. I used to play cricket, golf and swimming. My mother encouraged me to participate in anything and everything that I could possibly do.

"In the early seventies I became interested in snow sports when friends invited me to watch them ski. After watching for about five minutes, I went to a ski-hire place and got fitted up with the necessary gear. I went back up the hill decked out in all the latest equipment and proceeded to give it a go.

"The first time I went for about ten meters before falling over, and that is as far as I got. From then on in, I just kept standing up and falling down. But those first ten metres were enough for me to feel the wind going through my hair, and not being able to run, I had never had that feeling before."

Fineran was so enthused by what he felt that he gave up his sales job in Sydney and moved to a ski resort in Australia called Thredbo, where he continued to learn how to ski. Some ski instructors who travelled from Austria every year to teach in Australia told Fineran that they had seen amputees skiing on one ski with the help of outriggers, crutches with two little skis attached to them. Based on this description Fineran built himself a pair, and with the help of the Austrian instructors eventually was able to manage to ski short distances. He got a job at Thredbo and spent as much time as possible on the mountain.

In 1974, Fineran first travelled to Canada at the invitation of a Canadian who was a professional ski patroller at Thredbo, and who got Fineran a job working behind the counter at Grouse Mountain in Vancouver. There Fineran improved his skiing and was invited to join a group of disabled skiers travelling to Sunshine Village in Banff. He attended a disabled ski week with Jerry Johnston, then ski school director and now the head of Winter Sport for the Disabled in Canada. With Johnston's help, Fineran developed some proficiency.

Fineran recalls, "Having been taught to ski by Jerry, I advanced from there. I returned home to Australia, and travelled overseas once again in

1976 as the first ever Australian competitor in Winter Paralympics. I competed in the slalom and giant slalom in Örnsköldsvik, Sweden."

Fineran was given a scholarship to study physical education and recreation in Sweden, and stayed there until 1978, when he returned to Thredbo to once again take a job. In September, 1978, he and Bruce Able, a Canadian ski instructor, founded the Australian Disabled Ski Federation. They began to send teams abroad in 1980.

In 1992 Fineran got his first taste of international politics. As a member of the Alpine Technical Committee of the ICC he was instrumental in convincing the Tignes organization to maintain their commitment of timing for the 1992 Winter Paralympics. In Tignes the Australians gained their first winter gold medal in either Olympic or Paralympic history. The Australian team went on to greater heights in 1994 in Lillehammer with three gold, two silver, and four bronze medals. In 1992 Fineran was elected to head the Australian Paralympic Federation and was approached to put in a bid to the IPC on behalf of Sydney. The International Olympic Committee had told the Sydney Olympic Bid Committee that it would be highly advantageous for their bid to gain the 2000 Olympics if they put in a Paralympic bid as well. The Sydney Olympic Bid Committee offered to assist the Australian Paralympic Federation in putting a bid forward. Fineran says, "A separate bid was not acceptable as far as disabled sport in this country was concerned. We told them that we were not prepared to put in the bid unless they were prepared to cooperate fully with the organization thereof, as well of the 2000 games, should we get them. The organization of both the Olympics and the Paralympics Games should be a joint one."

During that period until the bid was announced in September, 1993, Fineran was involved in a great deal of hard-core political negotiation at international level. He found Bob Steadward's assistance invaluable. He says, "It was Bob Steadward's political manoeuvring and the way that he convinced people in Sydney, those people who were organizing the bid for the Olympics as well, that helped gain Sydney the Paralympics in the year 2000."

Gray Garner:
Great Britain

Gray Garner recalls refereeing his first wheelchair basketball game in 1968, when he was in the Royal Air Force. "My first impression was one of panic: 'Hell, these players move fast.' The second one was, 'How do you avoid the wheelchairs if you step on the court? Those E & J chairs ran about 45 pounds each, and were like tanks charging all around the gymnasium."

The friend who had talked Garner into officiating had promised that he'd be able to watch a couple of games before he'd have to blow a whistle. Of course no other officials turned up. But not only did Garner survive that tournament at Stoke Mandeville, he went on to referee internationally and coach the British team that won the first Gold Cup.

When Garner was stationed in Bahrain in 1970, he volunteered to work with disabled people needing physiotherapy. There he met Essa Alwatani, who had been through the Stoke Mandeville program after fracturing his spine. A shot-put champion at age 16, at 20, Alwatani was overweight and unfit, with no access to physical training facilities. Garner set up a training program for him, getting permission for Alwatani to use the RAF archery range, pool, shot put and javelin.

Six months later, when Garner was transferred back to Britain, Alwatani was fit and healthy, so healthy that he and his wife started a family. In 1979 Alwatani helped set up the first centre in Bahrain for people with disabilities, wanting to give others the help that he had received from Garner. These two were not to meet again until 21 years later, when, as vice president of Bahrain Mobility International, Alwatani came to the games at Stoke Mandeville.

Garner also had a huge impact on Arnie Astrada, an American shot-putter. In 1995 Garner was told Astrada was ill. He tried to contact him but couldn't, so sent him a letter.

Garner recalls, "I wrote, 'Get your act together, Arnie. Buck up. I missed you. There is nobody like you.' I took a picture of him at Barcelona and wrote on the back 'Who loves you, baby.' It seems he was very sick indeed, and this letter was like getting an injection in the arm. This letter stayed next to the bed, and when he got up in the morning, he would pick it up and re-read it. He never replied to me, and when I finally met him in Atlanta (he won a gold medal), he said to me, 'I couldn't reply. If I had replied to you, I'd have died. I wanted to reply to your letter personally, face to face. If it hadn't been for your letter I'd have been dead.'"

While Garner has helped hundreds of athletes as referee, coach and friend, another great contribution to disabled sport is his photography. He first took pictures in Heidelburg on a camera borrowed from the air force. He took two rolls of film, not realising until four or five years later how important those pictures were. Over the years he has taken hundreds of pictures chronicling the Paralympic movement, often at great personal cost.

Garner and his partner, Laura Friar, decided to photograph the 1990 Assen World Championships. He recalls, "We didn't think about asking anybody for financing. We financed that ourselves for about 1500 pounds. All we could afford was one double bed caravan that we hired in a little camping wood about 10 miles away, and it had seen much better days. We went with the athletes there, paid for food, paid for accommodation, paid for travel, paid for everything."

The pictures from those games were absolutely invaluable, because in 1992 Garner and Friar persuaded Royal Mail to sponsor the British Paralympic Association. Their trip to Assen meant pictures for posters, for magazines, for publicity. Without Garner's and Friar's sacrifices, that sponsorship might never have happened. Thirty years later, they are still financing their own trips.

Garner has little patience with photographers who know nothing about disabled sport. He says, "The angles for disabled sport are completely different. Everyone is looking at able-bodied when they first come in, with the camera angle about five foot nine inches, whereas with wheelchair sport the camera angle should be about two or two and a half feet. Otherwise we don't get the face, where the character comes through when they are competing."

Garner says, "The best thing about being a photographer for the Paralympics is meeting people I haven't seen for three years, five years, 10 years, sometimes 20 years. We are all one huge family. I have got something like four or five thousand brothers and sisters out there. Most of them are in wheelchairs, some are blind, some have CP, some have only got one leg. But they're all family at the end of the day."

Pat Griffin:
Canada

"When things are not going well, I tend to work harder."

Four-time Paralympian and veteran on the Canadian National Team, Pat Griffin started playing in 1978. He had been involved in stand-up basketball as a young person refereeing and playing, so when he saw his first wheelchair basketball competition, he decided this was the sport for him.

Over the years Griffin has seen a huge transformation in the sport. He says, "I think every Paralympics just keeps getting bigger and bigger, and basketball is certainly improving. There are more teams with a chance to win. In 1984, and a little bit in 1988, you were looking at maybe five teams maximum, but now I think you are looking at 10 to 12 teams.

"I guess the thing I find appealing is when you have an underdog go through a tournament and win. I have a lot of respect for Australia in the 1996 Atlanta Paralympics. They were ranked seventh or eighth going in, they had a lot of close games but they pulled them out, and they ended up winning the gold medal. If you were an Australian, you had to have goose bumps going up and down your spine because that was a phenomenal thing that they did."

Griffin sees this increase in the number of elite teams as springing from increasing bench strength. "Back when I first started playing, you might have one all-star class person on each team. The other team rolled and tried to shut down that one person, but now teams' starting line-ups might have four all-stars on them. It's a lot more competitive; you can't really key on one person any longer. The calibre of the game has come a whole long way in the last 10 or 12 years."

As an all-star player himself, Griffin knows well what it's like to have the opposition focus on him. "It changes your game in the sense that if you know the other team is gunning for you, you try to work better with your team-mates. Either they will be open, or you know they will be coming to help you so that you can get away from a double team. If your opponents are going to put more pressure on you, they have to take the pressure off somebody else on your team. So you hope that person comes through, and the other team pays for that decision."

Griffin expects more advances with teams from developing countries as their access to better equipment and training methods increases. "A team might have some good athletes, but when they are in 30-pound chairs to our 15-pound chairs, it doesn't matter how good they are. You don't have to be as good an athlete as the guy in a 30-pound chair; you can quickly go around him if you have a chair that is half the weight. More countries are holding basketball camps and training coaches better; once these teams are able to afford the equipment that we have in Canada and the United States, they are going to be much more competitive."

Pat Griffin's team-mates see him as a teacher, a leader and a motivator on his team. Typically modest about his impact on his team, Griffin says, "I think that I am not a real vocal person or a 'rah, rah' cheerleader type. It is difficult for me to be a cheerleader, or to say something magical. It's more what I do than what I say."

Griffin says there are many ways people, including non-athletes, can get involved in the disabled sport movement. "I have seen a lot of people who get injured or confined to a wheelchair who go through a period where they are a little bit defeatist, if you will, because they keep looking at what they did before and thinking that they can't do that, as opposed to what they still can do. In wheelchair basketball we probably do more travelling than most able-bodied players do. We have teams such as the Northern Lights, for instance, that travel all over Canada, as opposed to a lot of people playing recreational hockey, for instance, who probably don't travel outside of their immediate area."

Not everyone can be an elite athlete, but in addition to the recreational leagues, Griffin says, "If they have an interest in basketball but they are physically unable to play, there are always all kinds of teams that are looking for coaches, even referees; they could get into scorekeeping or work as a team manager. If you are looking at helping a wheelchair organisation, you can volunteer to work bingos, or do fundraising, telemarketing or school programs. There are all kinds of different things a person can do."

Rick Hansen:
Canada

"Sport is a vehicle to contribute to society."

Rick Hansen has devoted his life to improving the lives of those with spinal cord injuries. His *Man in Motion* tour of March 21, 1985 to May 22, 1987, during which he wheeled his chair around the world, raised over 20 million dollars for spinal cord research. Rick Hansen's gruelling journey set a standard for courage and determination that will likely never be equalled.

Hansen won gold, silver, and bronze medals in the 1980 and 1984 Paralympics and competed in the 1500m exhibition event in the 1984 Los Angeles Olympics. He believes, "All experiences in life shape our philosophy and the choices we make. Who we are is fundamentally based on those experiences. I feel very fortunate that my accident happened to me because it has given me a richness and quality of life. I feel very fortunate that I chose sport as a vehicle for me to do the things that I love. As a result of sport, I was able to be a world-class athlete. I achieved most of my athletic goals and dreams, and in the process had another dream: the dream of the Man in Motion Tour."

Hansen says, "Sport teaches you about the importance of having a dream and a goal. There can be setbacks, and sometimes you get beat. But the driving force, the motivation, is belief in your dreams, and belief in yourself."

Part of Hansen's success is that he constantly measures his progress against his own strict standards. He recalls the disappointment he felt at winning a wheelchair marathon world championship. "My personal goal was to be the first athlete to break the two-hour mark. When I came across the finish line first, I looked at the clock and my time was two hours, three minutes and 22 seconds. I started to rationalise it, saying, 'Don't worry about it, you've won a world championship,' but I didn't feel good about what had happened. My chair had been damaged in the air travel over and I hadn't bothered to check the chair. By not bothering to check it, I let myself down. In the eyes of the athletic world I was the world champion, but that situation was one of the most frustrating and disappointing events in my athletic career."

Hansen feels that true victory is winning for yourself. He says, "Sport has taught me there is more than just one winner in a competition. Even though somebody comes first, within each of the athletes is the personal triumph."

One of Hansen's greatest triumphs was an eighth-place finish. Two months before the qualifying event for the first ever wheelchair racing exhibition at the 1984 Los Angeles Olympic Games, Hansen crashed and dislocated his shoulder. He remembers, "I struggled with every fibre in my being to be there at the Olympic Games, and by some miracle, I managed to qualify eighth by one-one hundredth of a second. In the eyes of the world that's eighth position. But for me, it was one of the greatest athletic achievements in my life."

Hansen was the first person with a disability to participate in physical education at his university. He had the same motive then as he has now: he wanted athletes with disabilities to be considered and recognised in the context of athletics, with disability a secondary characteristic. He believes that elite athletes with disabilities should have a variety of choices to pursue excellence, and to compete in the best forum possible. Exhibition events in the Olympic Games extended good will and helped give athletes with disabilities recognition; denying full-medal status said to the world that disabled athletes weren't really athletes.

Hansen says, "Millions of people get messages about life through sport, and by denying athletes with a disability full-medal status, we are sending a dangerous message. These athletes are elite athletes first, and the physical characteristic is secondary, just like with an athlete who is over seven feet in basketball, or perhaps under five feet in gymnastics. Most sports have visible differences: between men and women, between weight classes, and so on. Since this principle of the level playing field is established in sport already, it is appropriate and warranted that athletes with disabilities be included in a separate event within a sport. These athletes truly deserve it."

Pat Heydon:
Canada

Pat Heydon started work in disabled sport in 1984 while working on her master's degree in Sports Administration at the University of Ottawa. She says, "Sport has been a part of my life since the day I was born."

Her volunteer job went from part-time, to full-time, to where she is today, a veteran planner, communicator, manager, diplomat and facilitator. She was director of Games Missions for two national and seven international multi-sport competitions, including the Winter and Summer Paralympic Games from 1992 to 1996.

Heydon says, "I don't look at it as sport activities for disabilities but rather involvement in sports. Whether it is people in chairs, or people who can't see, it's all sport."

Heydon is well aware that athletic success requires the right kind of support. She says, "When athletes train seven days a week, they can be and should be demanding of what product they get on the field, and how respectful we are of what they do. If they're going to put in all that time and energy, then they better get someone out on that field or pool who knows what they are doing. And they shouldn't put up with anything less than that."

While she believes that athletes with disabilities are athletes first, Heydon feels that one of the challenges for the CPC is dealing appropriately with the unique disabilities. She recalls an incident in Barcelona. "One of our sprinters, an athlete with a head injury, was having some trouble with two sprinters whom he had beaten who were taunting him, trying to get under his skin. In the last event, the 100 metres, our athlete turned around just before the finish line and pointed to them, as if to say, `Ha, ha I beat you again.'

"With that he took off on his victory lap with the Canadian flag, and these two Spaniards ran up beside him and were speaking to him. He turned around and started motioning all sorts of obscenities to them.

"Just at that point Samaranch walked into the stadium and the almost-capacity crowd was booing what was happening on the track.

"We were highly criticised upon return to Canada for sending a head-injury athlete home. On the one hand, we want to treat the athletes as athletes, and on the other hand, we have to contend with that sort of reaction when we do. That athlete does have a head injury, but was brought to the games with the knowledge that any inappropriate action would be dealt with severely. Having to deal with that almost forces you to re-evaluate the position that you take with respect to the athletes, and particularly athletes with head injuries.

"That becomes even more of an issue now with the inclusion of athletes with a mental handicap. Again, you have athletes who are perhaps not capable of rationalising their behaviour before it happens, or they may make the wrong decision in terms of how they are going to handle it. It has certainly added another dimension to our job of trying to establish a sporting tradition based on sport rather than disability."

This disparity in treatment of people with disabilities is a reflection of society, Heydon feels. "That is why I get so upset when I listen to various radio stations talk about 'disabled people' rather than 'people with disabilities' or 'people who are disabled athletes.' We must recognise them as people first.

"I think the defining line for me is when we look at athletes or individuals with a mental handicap. I don't think that the general population is looking at them as individuals, but as something 'special.' I use that word to mean almost anything you want it to be. But when we talk about athletes with a disability we are not talking about the disabled person, we are talking

about an athlete person. I think that is very difficult for the general population to understand.

"That is the difficult challenge we face. We need to recognise these people as individuals first, then look at what contributions they can make and what skills they have. In our particular case we have Canadians who are unique athletes who happen to have a disability."

Another challenge for the Paralympic movement is the involvement of women. Heydon says, "Certainly women are much further ahead than when I first started 15 years ago, but there is a long way to go. There is no question that there is a whole lot more work to be done, particularly at the international level, where women are tremendously under-represented."

Hans Lindström:
Sweden

"As a person who has been disabled, before you know what you can do, you have to reha- bilitate your thinking. Most health care systems take care of the functional rehabilita- tion, but sport rehabili- tates your mind."

A fine athlete himself, as an administrator Hans Lindström helped disabled sport move from rehabilitation to elite sport competition. He has worked tirelessly over the past thirty years to develop competitions that included athletes from all disability groups.

Lindström got into sports almost by accident when he was about twelve years old. He recalls, "I dearly loved one of the girls in my class in school. I heard that she went swimming one day a week, so I went down to the swimming pool and started to train for the same club. She didn't show up that week, so I had to go the next week. After those two weeks the trainer was impressed with my dedication and gave me a free card for the swimming pool. That's how I started."

As an able-bodied athlete, Lindström won national and international championships. After he lost a leg below the knee in a traffic accident in 1960, it was several years before he tried the swimming pool again, and found that he could still stroke and swim. Because there were few opportunities for him to compete as an athlete with a disability, he started to organise competitions for the disabled. Lindström says, "You might say that's still what I am doing, only I am not participating too often now."

Lindström coached the Swedish swim team for the Stoke Mandeville and Paralympic Games in the mid-1960's. Although he enjoyed this experience, he was disappointed that there were at this time no competitions for disability groups other than spinal cord injuries, and he disliked the "patient" atmosphere of the games. He says, "I had rather fresh experience from able-bodied elite sport, and thought that the difference between this and disabled sport competition was much too great."

Sir Ludwig Guttmann would likely have agreed with Lindström's description of himself as "obstinate from the beginning," as he and Guttmann disagreed on a number of issues, including functional classification. Guttmann believed that para- and quadriplegics should not compete against other disability groups. At one time he told people, "Hans Lindström is dangerous," because Lindström actively sought competitions that integrated the various disability groups.

Lindström greatly respected Guttmann's achievement, dedication, and integrity, but was frustrated with the technical problems in disabled sport competitions organised by the Stoke Mandeville organisation. He says, "It was no use to propose any improvements in the running of the sports; it was not received." In 1970-71 Lindström and a number of other coaches formed their own committee to improve swim competitions. Guttmann refused to recognize it, but the International Swimming Trainers Association for the Paralysed continued its work anyway, and a year later was accepted as the first sports committee in the modern sports for the disabled.

ISOD, the International Sports Organisation for the Disabled, formed in 1964, was supposed to do a better job of organising sports for visually impaired, amputees, and other locomotor disabilities. It took ISOD ten years to hold its first international competition (held at Stoke Mandeville); classification problems and the lack of qualified officials made this competition unsatisfactory. Lindström recalls, "It was at the 1974 Blind and Amputee Games in Stoke Mandeville when I one dark night went out on the grass where the field events were held, and swore an oath that I would work to make sport competitions for disabled athletes equally dignified as those I had experienced as an able-bodied elite athlete." He dedicated more than twenty years to fulfilling that vow. In 1979 Lindström was elected to ISOD, and then served on the executive of the International Coordinating Committee in its twelve years of existence.

Always a tough competitor, at 39, Lindström started training again. Amputee athletes could participate for the first time at the 1976 Torontolympiad. He recalls, "Although I was too old, I had been working for this for almost 18 years, and had to be a part of it." He won silver and bronze, as well as a gold medal in relay.

In the 1970's Lindstrom was one of a group of people who built a winter sports program for the disabled. The founders of the Winter Paralympics were not controlled by the disability orientation that the summer sports had. Lindström says, "We created a system based on sports, not on disabilities. We held the first world championships in 1972, and the first Paralympic Winter Games in 1976 in Sweden. Everyone organising the events worked for the sport, not for any particular disability."

Today as secretary general, SHIF (Swedish Sports Organization for the Disabled), and IPC Technical Officer, Hans Lindström strives to improve sport for athletes with a disability. His efforts have helped shape the greatest of all disabled sport competitions, the Paralympic Games.

Ljiljana Ljubisic:
Canada

"You can take life two ways. You can sit inside four walls, stick your head in the sand, and hope it will all go away, or you can get your boxing gloves on, put your dukes up, and take life on the best way you know how."

At the Seoul Paralympics Ljiljana Ljubisic was surrounded by swarms of fans, impressed by this 6'1" blonde, visually-impaired athlete who set world records in shot-put and discus. She got even greater adulation in Barcelona. "Because it was televised to a great extent, now I'll go to Europe, and will have people say to me, 'I saw you on TV; you were in Barcelona. You were so good.' That is so neat. It is something that we don't experience in Canada."

Ljubisic recalls how she got into competitive sport. "I think I was like most athletes with disabilities. I just needed an opportunity, and that came to me when I was dragged to a goal ball practice back in 1983. I fell in love with the sport."

She feels that sport for her "filled a huge chasm, where there had been lack of confidence and self worth, because I live in an able-bodied world where I wanted to be measured the same as others in a physical sense."

As with all athletes, Ljubisic's success is not without cost. "Any athlete that wants to compete as badly as I do is not going to have the family time you might want. You might not have the time to develop a financially rewarding career because you are so involved in putting all of your energy into sports. But I have done it willingly; it may be a struggle, but it is not a sacrifice."

Other people's sacrifices help shape Ljubisic's success. "My husband has given up all personal time after work, on weekends, and on holidays to support me, to drive me, to pick up every one of my discus and shot-puts. My coach is incredibly knowledgeable, and has dedicated to me a tremendous amount of personal time taken from her family and her career."

Ljubisic is concerned that with the success of wheelchair athletes in the Paralympic movement, other disciplines may be ignored. "Wheelchair athletes are only one-fifth of the disabilities represented at the Paralympics, and everybody seems to forget that in the education of the public. Our image is the person in the wheelchair, and there is nothing wrong with people in a wheelchair, but they are not representative of the other disabilities.

"I fear that the Paralympics are becoming the games for those who are least affected by their disability: the paraplegics, the high partially sighted athletes. The Paralympics are starting to lose some of the more disabled CP athletes, the totally blind athlete, the low-functioning quadriplegic athletes. The Paralympics need to provide opportunities for high-performance sports for all levels, not just for those who are least affected by their disability."

Used to being treated as an elite athlete held to the high standards of international competition, Ljubisic is bitter about her experience in Atlanta. "I can deal with the filth of my residence, the lack of food, the bad transportation, and no entertainment. What threw me into a six-month depression was that my sense of level playing field was chopped up and crapped on when officials did not use the same rule book to apply to all athletes in the field.

"In one case in my competition this lady chose not to be at first or second or final call; she should never have been allowed onto the field according to the rules. But the officials could not see beyond the disability to the high-performance athlete standing before them. One of the officials said to us, 'You know what, ladies and gentlemen, I feel that you are being far too harsh on this young lady. She has travelled a long way to be here today.' She

was allowed to compete."

Ljubisic's personal philosophy helped her work through the depression she suffered after Atlanta. She says, "I believe that all things happen for a reason. As soon as you get out of the victim mode of 'Why me, why did this happen to me, I'm disabled, I'm blind, I'm depressed, I'm poor, I'm whatever,' you can learn from these lessons that life has given you.

"I would challenge a person with a disability or with a difficulty to stop feeling sorry for yourself. Find that dream inside you and commit yourself to whatever it will take to reach it, whether you want to be a pianist, or an artist, or a mom who brings up her kids really well, whatever. Do the best you can with what you have been given."

Michael Massik:
United States

Two years ago Michael Massik knew almost nothing about the Paralympics. As executive director of the United States Fencing Association, what he did know was that there was a need for wheelchair fencing in the United States. Massik says, "As the governing body for the sport of fencing, we had an obligation to do something about that need. After we started the program, we found out there was such as thing as Wheelchair Sports USA, and in fact, that Wheelchair Sports USA has the over-riding governing authority for wheelchair sports in this country. Fortunately, they were delighted that we had taken the burden off them to implement a new sport. Our partnership works well."

The USFA integrates national level competitions for the wheelchair team and the able-bodied team. At any given time in the 30 different playing areas, some competitors are women, some are men, some are women in wheelchairs, and some are men in wheelchairs. Massik says, "Again, that is probably because we didn't know any different. We just said, 'Okay, you guys are a part of us now. Let go.'"

Fencing can be an excellent rehabilitation tool, and the USFA is exploring this area. Massik says, "You can participate in this sport from a wheelchair almost immediately after an accident if you have upper body motor control left, because there are no terrible physical demands like you would see in track, where you need to gain great facility in the use of a wheelchair. The wheelchair in this sport is incidental. It just happens to be two athletes sitting down."

Some Olympic fencers know this firsthand. USFA staged a wheelchair fencing demonstration with their Paralympic team competing against their Olympic team. The able-bodied fencers lost almost every contest. They were amazed at how quickly the wheelchair fencers had attained their high level of skill in this new version of the sport.

For Massik, the most meaningful part personally of the Paralympic experience was sharing Atlanta with his 14-year-old cousin, Adam Lan. Massik says, "It was extremely fulfilling for me to be with him at the Paralympics and have him see that, like him, there are a lot of people who take off their legs when they go to sleep. I think that for him it was a life-changing experience. I'm glad that I got to help him have that. I think that ultimately it will make him much more proud of the person that he is, and happy with the person that he is."

Adam says, "I felt kind of different from other people—not significantly, but every day I feel different from the rest. When I got to the Paralympics I felt that the athletes were like me."

Adam Lan

Adam's parents have worked very hard to mainstream him all his life, and he rarely had any exposure to anyone who was in a wheelchair, or who had a prosthetic limb. Being in the middle of all the athletes in the Paralympics was a learning opportunity. One concern he had was that he was nervous about going out in the rain because he thought that his prosthesis would attract lightning. Massik recalls, "He said to me, 'Think about it. People on the golf course get hit by lightning.' I said, 'Well, maybe you have a point.' We were lucky enough that we had talked to somebody who manufactures prosthetic limbs earlier that evening and he happened to be in the restaurant, so we went over and asked him if having a prosthesis means that you are more likely to be hit by lightning. He said no, and all of a sudden Adam's life was a little bit more open; he could go out in the rain now."

Adam's favourite event was sitting volleyball. Massik took him to a game, and Adam was immediately entranced. Massik arranged that Adam participate in a scrimmage after the day's competition ended, and recalls, "There were players from several different countries. They just embraced Adam; they taught him how to play, and they put him down on the floor. When you are good at a sport, you can make somebody who is very new to the sport also look good. These guys made him look like a champion, and he was just inflated with pride. They stayed there for more than an hour playing with each other, playing with him, and they were just very happy to be able to bring great joy to this new kid."

Adam has now started playing sitting volleyball; his goal is to go to Sydney. The Paralympics have made him aware of new possibilities. He says, "I have seen a picture of a skier with one leg, which really inspires me because I've always wanted to ski. I thought I couldn't, because my toes are up where my knee should be, and I don't have a knee, so it's hard for me to bend. Now I feel that I could ski; it's not another thing that is restricted from me. What Paralympians are doing is opening up doors for other kids. It is really the message behind the sports that matters: You **can** do it. Paralympians show that 'impossible' is only a figure of speech."

Reg McClellan:
Canada

"Everybody has a contribution to make in the life that we all live, and there is no better vehicle than a sport— for me, wheelchair basketball—to convey that particular message."

Gold-medal player, coach, manager, founder, organiser, administrator, advocate, Hall-of-Famer, web-page guru: Reg McClellan has done it all during 25 years in wheelchair basketball. Noted for his skill in making others believe in themselves, Reg never hesitated to put his team before himself. His comments about the player he admires the most reveal much of Reg's personal philosophy.

"Baruch Hagai from Israel is certainly in my mind the best all-round basketball player ever. I always looked forward to playing against him, to learning from the guy, and I always admired his tremendous talent. The biggest thing he had going for him, and I certainly tried to incorporate this in my game, is that he got the most out of every one of his team-mates. You could have a mediocre player playing with Baruch, and the guy would become a star, just because Baruch was able to see what that person's strengths and weaknesses were and do things in his own personal game that would cover up the weaknesses, and expand on the strengths."

Reg learned from his coaches, too. "As a relatively new player, the coach played me, much to the concern of some of the guys that had been around for a long time. They felt that the game was too close to put a new guy into that kind of situation. The coach just pulled everybody aside at a time out and said, `Listen, I'm coaching this game and doing what is going to be best for this team in the long term. Everybody has a contribution to make and has to support each other out there.'

"One of our best players rebelled. The coach had the strength to understand that it was best for that person to sit out, and adjust and grow in the game. Anyway, to make a long story short, I certainly gleaned a lot from that coach, and went on to play on the National Team." That coach was Bob Steadward.

Always an enthusiastic sportsman, Reg played, coached and managed hockey, softball, football and volleyball teams, and continued those roles after he got involved in wheelchair basketball in 1972; he has coached over 50 teams in his career. He founded the Alberta Northern Lights Wheelchair Basketball Society and acted as that team's first coach and general manager in 1976. Like many of Reg's achievements, this was not done without personal cost. He recalls, "We needed money in order to meet our commitments for the

NWBA that season. We needed to play in that particular league in order to grow and develop, as we didn't have a league of our own here in Canada.

"People were hesitant to play, and to put in that amount of time, and viewed it as a tremendous commitment when there was no money in the bank, so I went to the Capital City Credit Union and said we needed a bank account and $12000 in order to meet our needs for that particular year. We established the bank account, got a line of credit, and I used my house as collateral for the loan. We started fund-raising right away, and as it turned out, we never ever had a problem."

Reg has had many achievements in his varied career. He went back to school as an adult, earning a degree in social work while working full time. He brought the first ultra lightweight wheelchairs to the Canadian market in 1980, and worked on the Rick Hansen Man In Motion Tour. He became the first employee in wheelchair basketball at the national level in 1988 and is now the executive director of the CWBA. In addition to all his other accomplishments, he is an international classifier, has competed for 20 years in the NWBA, and has played in 24 national championships. As a player on the Canadian team, from 1974-1994 Reg missed only two competitions.

Chantal Benoit credits Reg with saving the women's program in 1989. "That was a crucial period for the program for woman. We finished fourth in 1988, and everything was not going as well as it was supposed to do. In 1989, when the basketball section was born through the Canadian Olympic Sports Association, Reg McClellan brought that program for women really alive, and changed every prediction that was made in 1988."

Reg has some vivid memories of competition. "Our first gold medal in '89 in Stoke was great because Gary McPherson, Dick Loiselle and Bob Steadward were all there. Those were the guys that were there back in the early 70's, that were cheering me on and supporting us when teams were beating us by 45-65 points."

Peter McGregor:
Canada

"What it really comes down to is your inner motivation. People can influence you, and give you the push in the right direction, but the onus is on you to actually get out and do it for yourself. You can't have the attitude that 'Oh, I'm in a chair—I'm screwed. So you have to get up and do it yourself."

Peter McGregor is a young basketball player with his eyes on the future. Peter's first sport was soccer. "I was born in Scotland," he says, "and I think soccer runs through the bloodline. Soccer is born into you. At eight years old I played my last soccer game. I was in a car accident and in a wheelchair, and when I got out of the hospital, my dad said to me that there were opportunities for me to play sports whether it be basketball or sledge hockey. I got into a chair that Reg McClellan let me borrow from the Lights, and the first person I played was Pat Griffin. He was just a phenomenal athlete, and up until this day he still is. If I can still put moves on guys when I'm his age, then I'll be laughing."

"Wheelchair basketball and the Paralympic games help a lot, not just with sport development, but they give disabled people a chance to get out and see the world instead of watching it go by. Society still has the attitude that you're in a wheelchair; what can you contribute? But there are always opportunities out there for the disabled to contribute to their community, whether it be through athleticism or another way. The more you get out, the more you just wheel in your chair—it doesn't have to be a sport—you are building muscle all the time just wheeling every day. If you can push that chair, you're three steps ahead of the game."

One of Peter's mentors is Cam Tait, a newspaper reporter and advocate for those with disabilities. Peter says, "He has CP. You have to have 30 years to listen really closely to understand what he is saying, but he communicates to people every day through the *Edmonton Journal*. He is a great authority about not only the disabled community, but everyday life."

Peter has clear-cut goals. He says, "Right now I am going to keep it simple: go to university, get an education, and play basketball. I got a scholarship to the University of Illinois; if it wasn't for basketball, I wouldn't have that opportunity."

Sydney is very much in Peter's thoughts. He is hoping to attend the Canadian national team's training camp, move up on the roster, and get a chance to be on a Paralympic or Gold Cup team. To that end he's being coached by Mike Frogley, National Team coach. But competition is fierce. Peter says, "With so many people out there, and new injuries happening every day, it's harder to compete in basketball. I think that there were 20-25 people in the national program ten years ago, and right now there are more than 60. Whether I am watching from the bench, or I am on the court, either way it would be a great achievement to be in Sydney."

Peter credits his father for much of his success in sports, and in life. "My dad has been a great motivator for me. If it wasn't for him, I would probably be looking out the window watching the world go by. He pushed, telling me, 'you can do better, you can do better. You have the skills, you have the ability.' I just can't thank him enough for that. I think—I hope that he is proud of what I have done."

He also credits the veterans with whom he shares the court. "These people have set the game so far ahead in Canada. I play with guys like Pat Griffin, Roy Sherman and Kevin Earl; the names go on. They take the time out to help you: 'You got to snap that wrist. You can wander down; you got to create a man advantage'—things like that. The help with your individual game leads you to the development of your team work."

Whether or not he ever achieves Paralympic gold, Peter will continue to play. "Just as long as the opportunity is there for basketball, if I can still play, I'll do it. Maybe I won't compete at the elite level or the national team level, but just going out to the gym and shooting hoops, just keeping active, I am going to be doing it until the day I die."

Gary McPherson:
Canada

"The best way to overcome the fear of doing something is to do it."

Gary McPherson reflects on his life in and out of disabled sport. "As a result of polio, I lived in the University Hospital for a total of 34 years. The advantage for me was that I got polio when I was young, so I didn't have a lot of history to compare before and after, and I think that helped me a good deal. I was always looking for what could I do next; how could I do it.

"I learned a lot in the wheelchair sport movement because sport for athletes with a disability is built around adaptation, either adapting to the sport, the equipment, or the attitude.

"I think being young allowed me to have the "I-want-to try it, can do" attitude rather than being a defeatist and looking back at what I would have been able to do before I got polio. I didn't have a lot of history, which I think was advantageous in that I looked forward and did things rather than looking back.

"The hospital was a great training ground for me. I learned about the academic world because the hospital is on a campus. I learned about politics, about people, about administration: how not to do things, how to motivate, to encourage people, to break rules, get around rules, change rules. The hospital was a great training ground in overcoming barriers, probably the best experience I could have had. My education is a unique blend of experience and knowledge.

"I've always loved to compete; I love the challenge and the fun. My roommates and I got recognised for doing the communication with the wheelchair games through amateur radio in 1968. I won virtually all the awards they have to give in my time with Jaycees [Junior Chamber of Commerce], such as the Rookie of the Year, and all our local public speaking competitions. Those were good for me even though they were a challenge, because my breathing muscles were paralysed as a result of polio, and I had to learn a technique called glossal phageal breathing, or frog breathing.

"I was also recognised for my voluntary work with wheelchair sport, winning most of their top awards. I've always believed that in order for disabled individuals to be included properly in the community, they need to be involved with everybody else. They shouldn't be singled out as being different, although we do have some unique and different requirements. If you think you're different, then you are. I think that attitude has been good for me.

"A real honour was when the University of Alberta Senate recognised me with an honorary Doctor of Law degree on November 16, 1995, and

I gave the convocation address as a result of that. I feel that instead of earning it at the university, I earned it through my efforts in the community. It is a recognition of what I've brought to the community, particularly on behalf of disabled individuals, but also in the community generally. It carries a significant responsibility; it recognises that I'm a representative of the university and respected by them.

"In 1988 the Premier's Council on the Status of Persons with Disabilities was formalised. Rick Hansen met with the provincial government when he was here on the *Man in Motion* tour. His ability to bring a profile to the issues of disability was the catalyst that caused the creation of this committee. I was the first chairperson; our mandate is to work for equal opportunity for Albertans with disabilities in order that we can be part of the mainstream of the province.

"When you're growing up in an institution you accumulate a lot of scars. I wasn't as impaired as a lot of individuals that live in that environment, but socially I was a little bit behind in my development in terms of relating to the opposite sex, being afraid to take risks in relationships, maybe even knowing how to do that. But I got married when I was 43 years old to my wonderful wife, Valerie. We have two children, Keiko and Jamie, seven and five. I've probably learned more in the last three and a half years about life and myself than I've learned in the last 35, simply because I believe that life is a life-long learning and self-discovery process, as is rehabilitation. I'm still learning to do things today that I could probably have done 30 years ago, but I just didn't know I could do them.

"Two things in life are great teachers: one is adversity, no matter what form it comes in, and two are kids. I've been blessed with both."

Anne Merklinger:
Canada

Dr. Steadward calls Anne Merklinger "one of the brightest people we've ever had in the sport movement."

Anne Merklinger has plenty of elite competition in her background. Winner of two medals in swimming at the 1979 World University Games, she was a great prospect for the 1980 Canadian Olympic team until the boycott of the Moscow Olympics was announced. Now she is aiming for the Olympics again as skip of a championship curling team headed for trials for the Nagano Olympics. Merklinger is also the first director general of the Canadian Canoe Association.

Anne's involvement in the Paralympic movement demonstrated her administrative gifts. She reflects on her work in developing the proposal for the structure of the umbrella organisation that would eventually become the International Paralympic Committee.

"There was no real democratic parent organisation for sports for athletes with a disability world-wide. We wanted to have the organisation be democratic, sort of grass-roots based and comprised solely of representation of member countries who elected their governing body, so all the member nations were totally of the direction that the organisation took, and they elected their officials to guide and lead them through each term.

"The community at large world-wide was ready to look at a new and different structure. We put together the structure, and identified a process by which the member countries could come together in what we call the founding congress.

"Canada was a leader in really creating the organisation, and it was only fitting that the person that provided the most leadership in our country for the movement at the time was Bob Steadward. So he was nominated and elected as president. There was a whole group of us: Bob, Rick Hansen, Gary McPherson and myself, who were really involved in getting the thing off the ground, and you can see where it has gone from there.

"I was hired by what was called the Canadian Federation of Sport Organisations for the Disabled, CFSOD, in '84, and I had been there a few years and had become very familiar with the whole international scene and the way in which decisions were made or weren't made. There was a real void of leadership internationally, and it was clearly what we all thought the community of persons with a disability needed to make things happen.

"Bob was president of the CFSOD at the time, and I got to work very closely with him by virtue of being executive director, so this was pretty well a shared vision, that and what later evolved for the inclusion of athletes with a disability, which is a subcommittee of the IPC. So I left the CFSOD and went to work for the sub-committee in '89-'90.

"There is always a European block, as there is in any amateur sport, because Europe traditionally thinks that it is the centre of the universe, and anything outside of Europe is secondary. But I think because Canada has really been a leader in the development of the organisation, there was such respect there that there wasn't a leader who could contest Bob's role as president. His leadership abilities are just far and away the best. There wasn't anyone who could even challenge him.

"I think that Canada is really respected for that, and for Bob as a person, and so it was actually pretty smooth—surprisingly so. I think it was due to the work we put into training the organisations, because there was a lot of work around developing the draft constitution, looking at the various models of government. We put a lot of time into those kinds of things and ran a pretty unbiased process, we felt, in looking for various candidates for those positions. Then it was the member countries who decided, so it was democratic. For once they saw the value in that.

"A very similar group of people have shared another vision in terms of having full-medal status events for athletes with disabilities in the Olympics. The last chapter in that one has not been written yet, but there has been a lot of progress made there, and we are still working hard on that one.

"There is enough value and merit in each event and its individual reasons for being, I don't think that anyone questions whether the Paralympics and Olympics will ever be totally amalgamated. I personally don't believe they should be. Each event stands on its own for its own reasons—some are assured and some aren't, and they don't have to stand the test of being measured up against one another. I don't believe they should be. One provides an excellent opportunity with athletes with a disability to compete in a segregated environment where they receive the profile they justly deserve, and the other is the same for athletes to compete in Olympic Games. What we are trying to accomplish is

where there is a select number of Paralympic events, events for athletes with a disability, to be rated on an equal basis or in the same context as in the Olympic Games, and I think we are pretty close to that."

Anne Merklinger receives great respect from her colleagues. Pat Heydon says, "Anne developed a good relationship with the Koreans. She went over on a couple of trips before the games and established a tremendous relationship with the organising committee to the point that I think that they truly respected her as an individual and saw past the barrier of her being a woman. There is still that respect there that is quite unique for the Korean culture."

Reinhild Möller:
Germany

Reinhild Möller is the first disabled athlete ever to receive a million dollar contract from a sponsor. Her achievements include medals in both winter and summer Paralympics.

Möller lost her leg at three years old in a farming accident. Her right hand was partly cut off, too, but was reattached. She had no problem getting adjusted to her prosthesis in the hospital and quickly returned home. Her parents treated her no differently than her sister; that, the farm life, and the able-bodied school she attended all helped her to grow up an active, healthy person. She did gymnastics at a sports club and was on the school team in basketball and volleyball. Then a doctor told her she must not do any more sports, because she supposedly had a bad hip. He thought she would over-strain it, need a hip replacement, and end up in a wheelchair.

Möller dropped out of sports. She recalls, "Suddenly I felt disabled. I never felt disabled before this. Because I thought that I had to be really careful with my body, I gave up my dream to be a physical education teacher and started apprenticeship as an optician. I got overweight and really unhappy." She went to a disabled sports club, started swimming and gymnastics, and then skiing.

She did so well her first winter that the disabled ski team invited her to a training camp at the end of 1979. In 1980 she competed at the Paralympics (then still called the Olympic Games for the Handicapped) in Geilo, Norway, winning a bronze medal in slalom.

Her success restored her self-confidence and she decided again to try physical education. She applied at the University at Heidelberg, passing rigorous ability tests to be accepted, tests which almost a third of the able-bodied applicants failed. In 1986 she got her master's degree in adapted physical education and sport science.

She recalls, "During that time, studying physical education in Germany was very much practically oriented. I had about 25 hours a week of practical training in all kinds of sports: cycling, track and field, basketball, volleyball and gymnastics; everywhere I had no problems. Sometimes my teachers didn't even realise that I had a artificial leg. To excel at Paralympic Games is the highest goal, but the biggest accomplishment for me was to be equal with the able-bodied students."

After earning her degree, Möller decided to travel around the world to study disabled sport organisation. She trained in the United States with the US Disabled Ski Team. She trained in New Zealand for three months and attended a national convention of disabled sports in Australia.

When she came home she continued to win medals in the Paralympics, and supported herself by giving slide shows about her trip. She took all sorts of jobs to try to survive, and then realised that able-bodied athletes at her level spent all their time training because they had sponsors. Möller began to write letters to companies to try to get sponsors. The amounts she got, small though they were, helped her to survive.

In 1994, when she was given about $1200, she decided perhaps it was time to stop ski racing and start thinking about retirement and the future. Lillehammer would be her last competition; since she'd started in Norway, she'd finish in Norway.

She came back with four gold medals, and her sponsor offered her a one million dollar contract, spread over seven years. Möller says, "For me it is not only a contract, but a responsibility to stay in disabled sports. I have to show other companies that sponsorship is worthwhile."

While she says Nagano will be her last Paralympics, Möller always finds excuses to stay in competition. She says, "Now the bigger challenge is not my disability, but my age. I try to get the message out that even when you get older, you can still compete. I am really thrilled when I see 80-year-old people in their helmets skiing down the course. My next challenge is to learn not to win any more. I have to learn to cope with being second or third or maybe sometime in last place."

Möller feels that too much emphasis is put on winning. She recently competed in able-bodied mountain bike championships in Germany, and was satisfied she'd done her best, even though she didn't place. She says, "We have a program in Germany called the Fair Play Program that teaches that sport is

not all about winning. Sport is meeting people, making friends, and feeling satisfied with your own body and with your own performance. Sports should be a lifetime occupation."

Barb Montemurro:
Canada

From organising closing ceremonies, to changing catheters, to serving on an international federation, to "borrowing" a car battery to power a friend's respirator: Barb Montemurro has done it all in her more than 20 years as a volunteer with disabled sport. As one of the people earliest involved in wheelchair rugby, Montemurro was thrilled to see it a demonstration sport at Atlanta, and a medal sport in Sydney.

In 1976 Barb Montemurro answered a small ad in her local newspaper asking for volunteers for the Toronto Olympiad for the Physically Disabled. Brought up in a family where, she says, "If you couldn't talk sports—leave," she was amazed that she'd never heard of disabled sports. She spent two weeks organising the Parade of Nations in the Opening Ceremonies, doing office work, being a "gofer," and working on closing ceremonies.

When the games ended, she volunteered with a sports club, the Toronto Bulldogs. Starting by refereeing wheelchair rugby, she went on to learn the rules and regulations of all the sports that wheelchair sports offered and became an administrator with the Ontario Wheelchair Sports Association. Some of her fondest memories are of taking teams to Stoke Mandeville.

Montemurro recalls, "At that point I had been involved for almost 11 years, and I really wanted to see where it all started. I had come to the foundation of the structure, where the Paralympic sports were invented, almost as if I had come home. What really struck me in Stoke was the spirit of everybody there. It didn't matter what anybody did: athletes, volunteers, people that served you the meal, coaches, officials, organisers. Everybody was an equal."

She was a team manager in Barcelona, and was awed by the scope of the games there, but by this time, her eyesight was almost gone. She says, "People have said that I had a pretty good attitude when my eyes went, and I think it's because of my involvement with all the athletes with disabilities."

Montemurro feels she's learned a lot about patience. She says, "If you can't do things quickly, the world will still go on. So it takes one and a half hours to load a team on an airplane. OK. No problem."

As a team manager Barb Montemurro has had her share of travel crises, some caused by airlines who had no conception of the organisation required to transport a team of athletes with disabilities. She vividly remembers one flight with 60 people in chairs returning from an international competition. Montemurro happened to look out the window of the plane and saw some baggage handlers had all the chairs out on the tarmac, and were taking all the wheels off and throwing them into a bin. The team's equipment people dashed off the plane and ran out to stop them, with all the security personnel running after them. Barb says, "I really didn't care that we were not supposed to be in that secured area; I just thought about the nightmare when we got home if any more wheels went into that bin!"

Montemurro is astounded sometimes by the lack of understanding shown by questions people ask her, like how come membership numbers are declining in many disabled sport organisations. She says, "I told them that we are probably one of the few organisations that would some day like to be out of business, because we would be quite

happy not to have any wheelchair athletes. If you want more numbers, I said, then we will just put the diving board in the shallow end of the pool, we will get rid of the Mothers Against Drunk Driving program, we will get rid of the seat belts. That's recruitment, right?"

Cato Zahl Pedersen:
Norway

I like challenge in sport: to get a little bit better, day by day. You learn your strong side, and your weak side."

Cato Zahl Pedersen began his athletic career after an accident with high voltage that resulted in the amputation of his arms. From 1980 to 1996, he received 13 gold medals in alpine, cross-country, and track and field. In 1994 he went on an unsupported expedition skiing to the south pole with two other Norwegians, Harald Hauge and Lars Ebbesen.

While his companions had experience from expeditions in Greenland and Norway, Pedersen had none. He says, "But before my accident I had never been without my arms, either, and I think I do that quite well. So why not try another challenge?"

Each of the three men pulled a sledge carrying 265 pounds of food and equipment. Pedersen had some difficulty with the prosthesis on his right arm and his left arm is completely amputated, but he still managed to ski ten hours every day for 54 days. They did 700 miles from the sea of Antarctica to the south pole. The temperature went down to -45 at nights, and with strong winds at times was down to -70. Pedersen recalls, "The most difficult part was a stretch of about 150 miles that looks like an ocean in frozen ice in very hard wind. It was waves all over and very hard to get through."

That experience taught Pedersen much about himself. He says, "I learned you have a lot of energy, more than you think you have when you give it a chance. You learn to be patient. You learn to not hurry. You learn to believe in yourself. You also learn that success depends on believing you can do it."

Pedersen feels that his Paralympic experience was of great help to him. He recalls, "The team feeling is the most important thing. We said to each other before we left that it is more important to be friends after the expedition than to reach the goal. We helped each other a lot, not so much in the physical way, but in the mental way of helping each other through bad days."

This expedition had no chance to fail, Pedersen says, because they had no communication with the world, other than a daily message sent by satellite, with no way for the team members to know whether or not their transmission got through. He recalls, "We were alone, and had to believe in ourselves."

Humour helped the three men survive. Pedersen recalls Christmas Eve, 1994, when they cut a big cake in three equal pieces. He recalls, "We wanted as much cake as possible, because we were very hungry. At the time Lars was looking at me and said, No hands, no cake!"

They ate 7000 calories a day, including heavy foodstuffs like butter, chocolate, almonds, and packaged frozen dinners with a lot of calories.

The men used about 9000 calories a day; Pedersen lost about 40 pounds in two months.

Cato Pedersen's Paralympic career began in 1980. He competed in Geilo in cross country, slalom and giant slalom, winning three gold. In Arnhem, 1980, he competed in 100 metre, 400 metre, 1500 metre and long jump. In 1984 he competed in New York, winning the 1500 and 5000 metre, and in 1988 in Innsbruck, in Austria, he won the giant slalom and double needle. In 1994 in Lillehammer he won the giant slalom, the super g, and silver in the down hill.

Pedersen says, "In Norway we were accepted as top athletes together with the Olympic family; there were very good combined arrangements between the Olympics and Paralympics. The support for the disabled sportsmen was wonderful, but I have a lot of good friends on the Norwegian able-bodied team that we practise with, and they say they are motivated by seeing us without poles, or on one ski, and seeing how well we ski. They get inspired by us."

Pedersen wants to see the Paralympic and Olympic movement as one family, although he doesn't see the competitions necessarily being joined. He says, "All athletes should have the ability to compete in equal ways and the ablest will be in the Olympics. The Paralympics are a great expression to the rest of the world that people with disabilities have the same enjoyment and the same challenges in sport that the able bodied have. I know a lot of national and international athletes in the Olympic movement who are very impressed and very interested to have us move closely to their movement. That is also something to do with the national organization. In Norway, we are working now for one organization for able-bodied and disabled sport."

Donna Ritchie:
Australia

Always look at what you can do. Focus on that, and not on what you can't do.

Donna Ritchie played a lot of able-bodied sports, so it was natural for her to get into wheelchair basketball after becoming a paraplegic as a result of a fall in 1987. Her family's love of sport played a big part in encouraging Ritchie's sporting achievements; her father played league rugby for Australia. The idea of competition and being the best you possibly can be has always been part of her life.

Ritchie says, "My aim is to be the best I can be as an individual, and then be the best within a team. You have to think about your role in the team. My role with my level of disability is not trying to take on, say, Chantal Benoit, because she has far more function than I do. She would just burn me. In able-bodied basketball everyone can do everything: they can hop, skip and they have all the balance, whereas in the Paralympics, with the functional classification, it is a lot different. I really psych myself up and think about the moves that we have, what we have got to do to get out of those nervy situations. But I think of the team as a whole, and then about how I will play myself."

Like all great players, Ritchie knows her limitations and works around them. She says, "With my level of injury my balance isn't probably as good; I fall out sometimes and do some stupid things. I think that you just have to laugh at yourself; otherwise you start taking things too seriously.

"I know I can't jump. I don't want to focus on that. I want to focus on what I can do. Whether you are able bodied or you have a disability, there are always challenges. It's how you cope and adapt to these challenges that makes all the difference. You really only get out of sport what you put in. For me it is very satisfying to put in the hard work and see results. When you see improvement, being competitive is a fantastic feeling."

Ritchie's first international competition was in Japan in 1989; her first Paralympic Games was Barcelona. She recalls, "When I wheeled out and I saw how crowded it was, all the support and the flags and everyone happy and waving, I thought, *Oh, I am here at the opening ceremonies of the Paralympic Games. I have done it. I have worked really hard to make the team.* Actually making the team was more fantastic than being there. It was a very proud moment."

Her team finished fourth, and she left Barcelona feeling she had to work harder. She says, "Fourth is not good enough. Yes, it's lovely to just get there like everyone says, but hey, I would like a medal."

More disappointment waited in Atlanta. The Australians lost their bronze medal match. Ritchie says, "I felt really down with myself, down that we didn't finish higher. I had to come away and look at what I was doing. How could I improve? Did I want to put all the work in toward 2000, with that fear of coming away with a fourth or fifth place? It is really hard working for something for four years and then it is over within a few days, and that dream that you had is now gone again."

Ritchie's ambition burns passionately again now. She says, "I came away and I thought, I don't think I'm up to the fullest of my potential. I think that I can still learn. I think that I can still make a valid contribution to the team."

Of course the fact that the next Paralympics will be held in Australia influenced Ritchie's decision. She says, "I am a very proud Australian. I look forward to inviting the athletes of the world to Sydney. I think the Paralympic Games are going to go to a new height in the year 2000, and working so closely with the Olympic Organizing Committee, we have some great benefits here."

Ritchie wastes no time worrying about inequalities between able-bodied and disabled sports. She says, "I think you have got to keep it in perspective. The Paralympic movement is a lot younger than the Olympic movement. We are growing, but our time will come. Sydney 2000 is the twenty-seventh Olympiad, but only the eleventh Paralympiad. Did the eleventh Olympics have the number of winners and the recognition that the twenty-seventh will have? No, of course not. We need to show the media and the public the results our athletes achieve, and, in 2000 the crowds will be there supporting us."

Marie-Claire Ross:
Canada

"You know in your heart it takes sacrifice to get where you want to go."

Marie-Claire Ross is the first woman with a disability to qualify for a national championship in Canada: the Canadian Intervarsity Athletic Union (CIAU) Championships. Top swimmers from universities across Canada and the US compete at this final championship meet.

While Ross is pleased with her accomplishment, she says, "The big thing for me is swimming the faster time, continually improving and getting stronger. Whether I am competing against people without sight or not doesn't really make a difference for me, but I know that a lot of other people find this rather inspiring. So I sort of got into the mood. I am really excited about it."

Ross is a little baffled by all the attention from the media. She gets some interesting comments and questions. "A lot of people, reporters and media, and even some people I have met that didn't know that I was legally blind say, 'Wow, like you wouldn't know. You act like you're normal.'"

Ross works hard to minimise the effects of her eyesight, simply because, she says, "It's a lot easier and less distracting for people if you look them straight in the eye. When I look at people, I can't actually see them, but it is still important for me to try to point my face to make eye contact."

The first question most reporters ask is about how she makes turns. She answers, "There is a black line that travels along the bottom of the pool, and a 'T' that marks the coming of a wall. I can see that. I don't have depth perception, so when I'm looking straight in front of me, I can't judge exactly how far I am away from the wall. I also count my strokes, so I have a very consistent stroke rate. I use a combination of those two things to gauge my turns; I do have weak turns. When you are swimming fast, and you feel like "Oh, where am I," it's sometimes hard to swim confidently into the walls."

Ross began swimming at age 15. She recalls, "I have always loved the water. I think I got into swimming sort of as an alternative, because I had difficulties doing any sort of sports that involved balls, and running around, and interaction like team play, because I just couldn't see well enough to do those things."

Asked about her training strategy, Ross says, "You have to have a goal. If you are training for a specific set of games or to reach a certain time, and you are committed to that goal, that's very empowering. Sometimes you just say 'I have to do this,' because basically, when you wake up at 5:00 o'clock and have to train for two hours, some mornings are torturous."

This dedication paid off for Ross in Atlanta. She recalls her six gold medal ceremonies. "It's probably different for everyone, but I just soaked it up. It was my moment. I wasn't thinking about the past. I wasn't thinking about the future. I just tried to soak it all in: the way I felt, the way my clothes felt, my jacket, and the medal hanging around my neck, the light, the sound of the anthem, the sound of the people in the stands. This was what I had worked for, and I was going to experience it."

The Paralympics have helped Ross grow as an athlete, and as a person. She says, "Barcelona was wonderful for me. It revolutionised the way I felt about sport. I was a rookie, not confident at all in competing; I had a lot of reservations with regard to my eyesight, and I felt I

was limited in certain ways. That experience has really changed my perspective because I saw so many fabulous athletes there who are confident and proud of their achievement and of who they are, regardless of what body parts they are missing, or whatever. I think through sport a lot of people are able to achieve that positive spirit, that confidence in themselves."

Ross, already a world-record holder in her events, has people tell her that she is moving up now that she is competing against able-bodied people. She responds, "Well, my times are continuing to improve, and I am getting stronger, but I don't view it as moving up. I am ecstatic about my personal progress, about moving into a realm of people that will continue to push me to swim to improve, and to train harder, and become a stronger swimmer. But in terms of competition, I don't view the Paralympics as a lower level of sport."

Eric Russell:
Australia

"I fully credit wheelchair sports with allowing me to re-establish my identity, to measure myself against others of similar types of disability."

In 1976 the Canadian government withdrew support from the Paralympic Games in Toronto because South Africa had been invited to compete. Eric Russell recalls, "I refused to accept the first medal I won in Toronto to protest the involvement of government politics in disabled sports. I didn't do it in support of South Africa. My protest was based on my belief that we had enough of a common bond within our disabilities without governments trying to use us for their own political ends."

Russell recalls an interview with an irate Ludwig Guttmann, who told the Australian team to send Russell home on the next plane. The Australians replied that if Russell left, they would all leave. Bob Jackson, Canadian organiser of the Games, stepped in as peacemaker, and pointed out that Russell's protest echoed Guttmann's own feelings on the subject of politics and sport. In the end Guttmann supported Russell's action.

Russell was often controversial in his 20-year career, usually because he was trying to make conditions better. He found the competition at Stoke Mandeville very rehabilitation-like in its attitude, not surprising given the history and nature of those involved. Russell felt that the organisers needed to become more professional in their administration of the sport, and remembers, "It was difficult to find the rules; they were all in someone's head." He recalls breaking a world record in 1975 in shot-put while shot-putting downhill. At the same time a friend from New South Wales was trying to break the world record in discus, throwing uphill.

In 1978 Russell became chairman of Athletics of the Wheelchair Sports International Federation. He says, "All of the goals that I had set for the athletics organisation, such as controlling and sanctioning our own events, being in control of our own world records, being in control of our rules, and of the organisation of major international games, goals that I had set in 1978, I had achieved by Seoul in 1988."

Russell's wife, Julie, competes in athletics and weightlifting. They find that life with two elite athletes in one house can be challenging. Eric says, "The main advantage when you are married to an athlete is that you understand what an athlete has to do in terms of diet, and lifestyle, and sleeping, and not wanting to go out late, and spending massive amounts of time in training. There is an understanding that you will be away for long periods of time. There is an understanding that it will cost you heaps and heaps of money out of your own pocket." In the 10 years Russell was chairman of Athletics, he and his wife spent nearly $35,000 of their own money on air fares.

Russell sees another disadvantage to athletes sharing a house. "Top-class athletes become very focused, very moody, and if you have two athletes in the one house, there is likely to be conflict about competitions, and who needs support right there and then. It can become a little testy."

Attitudes since the early days of his career have changed tremendously, Russell feels, not only in sport administration, but also in the public. He says, "In those days, people used to say things like 'Oh, isn't it wonderful that they can compete,' with the emphasis on the 'they.' We weren't seen as people, we were seen as rehabilitees, and the general public just thought it was 'wonderful.' In this day and age, wheelchair athletes are recognised as athletes in their own right."

Russell had to battle his own attitude. He played rugby football at the top levels before his accident. He recalls, "When I broke my back, I was transferred to the spinal injuries unit in Brisbane, and I remember distinctly the second day I was there looking at a notice up above my head. It had in big writing my doctor's name, and in very little writing my name. I thought to myself, 'There's the sign of the times. I am no longer the important person; my doctor is. Suddenly, I didn't know who I was any more. I had lost everything in terms of personal identity. I fully credit wheelchair sport with allowing me to re-establish that identity, to measure myself against others of similar disability. It gave me the encouragement to go back into the world as a person in my own right."

After achieving his administrative goals, Russell returned to competition, setting a world record in javelin in 1990. Throughout Russell's career, he continued to battle negative attitudes to earn better conditions and more recognition for athletes.

Alana Shepherd:
United States

Alana Shepherd recalls how the Shepherd Centre got started. "My son had a body-surfing accident. He was lucky enough to have an incomplete injury, so he walks with a leg brace and a crutch. During all of that long time that he was in three different hospitals, we realised once we found spinal care at its highest level that this was really fabulous, such a difference from fine medical care in a general hospital."

The Shepherd family decided that a spinal care treatment centre was needed in Atlanta so that people would not have to travel in search of proper care, or indeed not be able to find it. The Shepherds found a medical director with the proper training in spinal care, plus support from the community. "Because it was so needed, it just took off from that point," Shepherd says. "We went from six beds to the 100 we have now, with 25 or 40 patients in the day hospital, and almost 3000 multiple sclerosis patients under treatment."

While sport is part of the rehabilitation program, it is not for everyone. The Shepherd Centre has a recreation department with specialists in other areas, such as drama, art and music, with even a horticultural therapist on staff. Mrs. Shepherd says, "The dimension is there no matter what your age or your inclination. Everyone can't and isn't going to be an athlete. We know that. To want to return to work, to school, to running your house, to being an active member in your community: that is the challenge."

Initial consternation when the Paralympics weren't included in the Olympic bid turned to determination for Shepherd. She says, "The struggle within the groups to back it, to get everybody excited about it, to have it accepted, and then put it on: that was an incredible experience." The Shepherd Centre backed the bid and then provided APOC with funding.

The Paralympics inspired many at the Shepherd Centre. Shepherd says, "Our in-patients realised what was possible. After seeing that high level of achievement the Paralympic athletes demonstrated, some of our former patients have become sports enthusiasts, trying different sports. So many have said, 'I realise now that there are so many things that are still possible, and I can do it at a better level than I ever thought I could.'

Although she wishes that more people had attended the Paralympics, Mrs. Shepherd continues to hear from people who were thrilled by the calibre of the competition. When these people ask her, "Why wasn't there more on television?" her response is, "Where was your voice then?"

Another aspect she continues to field questions about is the pull out of six Olympic sponsors who declined to sponsor the Paralympics but did not allow other companies to take over their sponsorships. She says, "It was a great marketing technique on their part: they could keep their competitors out of something that would have been wonderful, and they didn't have to pay any money. People send me copies of the letters that these corporations write a lot of times, and they are saying, 'Actually, we did release our categories.' They did not! To me that serves to say 'We missed a grand opportunity, and we will find opportunities in the future to support sports for the disabled.'

Mrs. Shepherd believes that the Paralympics have left a legacy in Atlanta, a city already committed to being accessible for the disabled and placing them in jobs. She says, "Atlanta is different than other parts of our own country, and that legacy is continuing to grow. It was here anyway because the Shepherd Centre sends its patients in every direction; our buses are visible at every sporting event, every concert, every festival. Then there is the wheelchair division T3 road race, which we have sponsored from the beginning. People are just aware of people with disabilities."

The effects are also seen beyond Atlanta. Mrs. Shepherd says, "We know of a university in south Alabama that has hired a staff person to be in charge of sports for the disabled. Schools are beginning to realise that they better not send these students to study hall instead of physical education; they can play with everybody else outside, and rough-house around, and they're not going to break. That's healthy, and that's the way it should be. Those perceptions are the things that are changing with the legacy of the Paralympics, and that makes me feel very special."

Randy Snow:
United States

Randy Snow, elite athlete in tennis, track and basketball, is the first Paralympic athlete to hold medals in three separate sports during three different Summer Games. Now his proudest accomplishment is his success in changing his focus from always striving to win and validate himself to taking pleasure in seeing others win. He spent the first part of his tennis career beating everyone, and now he's teaching everyone to play the game. Snow says, "I've studied what it takes to win, and now I demystify the instinct and give it to somebody else."

At 16 Snow was a nationally ranked tennis player. Then he was injured in a farming accident when a 1000-pound bale of hay damaged his back. His large family (he has five younger sisters) was critical to his recovery. He recalls, "My family was smart enough to draw the line. A lot of families enable and help too much. Life should be a struggle; that's what makes us survive. I went through the normal stuff like anybody else of not accepting it and fighting it, hanging on to the initial coping mechanisms of angry denial and depression, rather than going on to acceptance."

Snow uses his recovery experiences to help others adjust to disability. His company provides people with equipment to enhance mobility and independence. After 20 years of counselling people through their recovery period he still can be deeply affected by what he sees.

Snow says, "We have a guy now whose wheelchair my company, Allumed, is doing. He retires at 56, and buys himself a Harley as a retirement gift. Three miles down the road from the motorcycle shop on his way to his new home in Sun City, he crashes and breaks his neck. I have been to his house and seen the sadness, the fear and the scepticism in his face. I just want to let him know he is going to be okay. Of course he doesn't see it. The blinders go on. You only see it one way; you see the things you can't do anymore. But as you get further into your injury, those

"I really dig being in a wheelchair. If God told me, "Snow, you made it; here are your legs," I would go, "You know, God, there is the European tour next year in tennis, and there are girls that really like me because I am in a wheelchair . . . . Do you mind if I just hold off for about a year? I want my legs but just let me cruise for a little while longer."

blinders retract, and you can start to see things that you can do. That single vision of who you were becomes irrelevant. Time is the only thing that allows you to realise that."

Snow was part of the movement to get wheelchair tennis accepted as a Paralympic sport. He's proud of the impact the tournaments, exhibitions, clinics and camps run by the Wheelchair Tennis Foundation have had, training hundreds of players at all levels of age and ability.

Although he only plays able-bodied players now in exhibition matches, Snow enjoyed competing in able-bodied tournaments. He says, "I don't even see an able-bodied person; I see a quick athlete. I let some balls go way back in, and especially way down low. It's automatic, like you're playing a fast and tall wheelchair player, so you try to negate that. It's pure athletic perspective rather than philosophical or cultural."

Snow vividly remembers the exhilaration and pride he felt in Barcelona. He recalls, "Man, you train four years, and you go to Barcelona, and that stadium is full. They're waving those hands and you are overrun, like a window to your soul opens and pours the stuff out all over you. You have to stay humble, but you can't help but sit there and go 'Yes!'"

Ellen Stohl:
United States

"The package we come in doesn't define who we are. It's the spirit that prevails within us."

Motivational speaker, actor, model, activist: Ellen Stohl inspires all who meet her. Her achievements range from convincing *Playboy* that it was time to feature a woman in a wheelchair, to earning a master's degree in psychology, to working on the development of a team-building physical endurance program to be led by people in wheelchairs.

Ellen's greatest strength is her global view of disability and its place in society. She says, "Disability is going to happen to everyone. A recent study done by the Institute of Medicine says that on average every American will experience a disability in their lifetime. The Paralympics to me are a celebration of the fact that no matter what level you are functioning at, you can find a way to achieve excellence. This means it isn't about a separate group; it's about all of us. Watching people achieve greatness despite differences or perceived obstacles gives us the opportunity to see the potential we all have.

"To realise that people with disabilities are just people pursuing goals and dreams is empowering, not just to people with disabilities, but to the whole community at large, because everyone has some sort of disability they are dealing with. Whether it is psychological, a family issue, an emotional issue, or a physical issue, everybody feels less than perfect. When you see someone who has a visible disability striving to achieve greatness, it taps into you that 'Wow, they're doing it. I can do this. My life can have greatness. I don't have to be perfect to live life with passion and power.'

"Our media is geared to bombarding us with unrealistic images of how we should look, how we should be, and if we don't somehow live up to that, we're less than OK. To see people who visibly don't meet those standards but who are living their lives and going after whatever it is they desire: that taps into us. 'Wow, you know what, I can have these things too. I am deserving. I can do it.' I think that is so empowering, and I think that all society would benefit from seeing more of it.

"Kareem Abdul Jabar talked to me about how difficult it was to be so tall. He was stared at, he couldn't get into cars, he had trouble in airplanes. People made fun of him when he was growing up. It was devastating until he learned to find a way to use his height to an advantage.

"A disability can seem like an obstacle, but in truth it is a opportunity to learn more, to find out what you can do. You may not be able to control the circumstances in your life, but you can control what you do about them. Paralympic athletes are the cream of the crop, just like Olympic athletes. But their pursuit of excellence is simply an example that we can pursue any dreams we have, whether it is racing down a road, getting a job, or going to school.

"There is a great shame and stigma attached to disability in our society. Nobody wants to be disabled. If you ask anybody, they are not going to stand up and say, 'Choose me, choose me.' The historical perspective of disability is that to create the ideal society, the deformed should be locked away. During the Third Reich over 200,000 people with disabilities were killed as a form of treatment, and their families were billed.

"It's hard for the general population to realise that they create this paternalistic view that those with disabilities are somehow less fortunate, and I don't know that we are less fortunate. We do face greater obstacles, but those obstacles can be erased by creating a universal society. I don't think about my disability until I can't get in somewhere, until somebody stares at me, or until somebody says to me, 'If that happened to me, I'd kill myself.' When somebody pats me on the head, or treats me like I'm an idiot, or talks to my partner instead of me because they think I can't order my own food: those are the things that make me feel 'less than,' not the disability.

"Education is the key. Once we see more people with disabilities as mothers, fathers, engineers, dentists, athletes and lovers, and partners and teachers, we begin to see that who they are is not the disability, and I think the media is the key to that education. If the Paralympics had been on television more, if we had sponsors using more athletes in the commercials along with Michael Jordan—the dream team and the wheelchair team—if we could see more similarities than differences, then people would realise that we are more alike than we are different."

Walter Wu:
Canada

"If you have a goal, and you have the discipline to carry it out, that attitude you put towards sport carries over into how you should work, how you should basically live the rest of your life."

Winner of six medals at the 1996 Paralympics, Walter Wu initially found life in Atlanta difficult. He says, "The first couple of days I was nervous: with 3500 athletes here, this was a big deal. I heard that 60,000 people were at the Opening Ceremonies, and that means other people think it's a big deal. I was a big ball of nerves until I got my first swim over with. Once I did that, those 10 days just went by. We ate breakfast, we swam; we ate lunch, we swam; we ate dinner: that's how our life went for 10 days. I loved every minute of it."

Wu won the 400m freestyle in 4:21.08, 11 seconds faster than the previous world record, but takes great pride in his team-mates' achievements. He recalls, "Marie Claire Ross lived at my house for three months and trained with me this summer. She always swims right after me at these international meets; we are quite close. One of my proudest moments was on day two of the swim meet. Her whole family was in the stands, I had just won the 200 IM, she went into the 200 IM right after me, and she broke a world record by about three seconds. She was waiting for this moment for two years, and I was so happy for her when it happened."

"A Paralympic athlete is not doing it for the money," Wu says. "She gets no endorsements after winning all these medals. She does it for the pure love of the sport. If we do well, it is just an honour for us and our country. The only time money is a factor with us is when there is not enough of it to support us. I know a lot of the swimmers that went this summer had to pay their own way. I think that's wrong. We should have at least enough money that none of us have to pay to get there."

The Paralympics make Wu want to encourage more people with disabilities to get involved in sport. He says, "I would tell them some of my experiences: how people want to talk to you, to learn about you. You shouldn't be afraid to open up to them. They're not going to laugh at you. They are actually quite proud to be in your presence, to see someone with this disability do something that they themselves might not be able to do."

Wu's biggest inspiration is his family. He wants to show his parents that their support resulted in something good for their son. In 1994 his sister made the Canadian Commonwealth Games Swim team. Wu says, "I thought, well, my sister can do it. I have the same genes as her, I know I can work as hard as her, and maybe I can achieve the same goal as she did."

Other swimmers were important too. He recalls, "I grew up in the era when Alex Baldwin and Victor Davis were kings, and watching how well they did in 1984 was one of my big springboards to swimming. Hey, Canada is good at this stuff: those two are very good mentors for me.

When I met them they both gave off this confidence, just in their walk, how they carried themselves. They had confidence in their abilities. I hope one day I can be like that."

Sometimes able-bodied swimmers have difficulty believing Wu can beat them. He says, "I have had a couple of instances where people didn't believe I was disabled. I remember at one swim meet they had results posted on the wall, and I had my face plastered against it trying to read it. Until this one competitor saw me doing this, he didn't believe that I was blind. When he saw that his mentality changed. It wasn't compassion; he was not disappointed in his own actions, but just was impressed by what I was able to do."

Wu was impressed by some comments from Donovan Bailey, winner of the 100m at the Atlanta Olympics. "Donovan asked one of my friends what sport did he compete in, and he said, 'Paralympic track athlete.' Bailey got quite upset at him and said, 'Do you train hard?' My friend answered, 'Yes, I do.' Bailey asked, 'Do you sacrifice yourself to train?' 'Yes, I do.' Bailey said, 'Then you are not a Paralympic athlete. You are an Olympic athlete.' Coming from Donovan Bailey, our most successful athlete this summer, that was a big thing to hear."

Wu says, "I think that Canada is a lot different than the rest of the world: athletes are athletes."

Duncan Wyeth:
United States

"It is important to each and everyone of us to express ourselves, not in terms of what we can't do, but in terms of what we can do."

Teacher, Paralympian, administrator, public servant, speaker on disability issues: Duncan Wyeth attributes much of what he has been able to accomplish to his supportive parents, who actively encouraged him to take risks. Wyeth says, "I did not have some of the learned passivity that some people growing up with cerebral palsy would have had instilled in them. I always had encouragement from my family to try to be the best that I could be."

Wyeth's parents did not want him in a segregated learning situation. He was the only child in his neighbourhood junior and senior high schools with any physical disability. He played intramural sports against nondisabled athletes, and was manager of a high school basketball team and track team. His friends tended to be athletes themselves, athletes who did not have disabilities. Later he joined a cycle club whose members made him feel welcome and took time to give him pointers on improving his technique.

When Duncan was 14, the family lived for two years in Taipei, where his father taught at the University of Taiwan. As a result, he says, "I had an attraction to international exchange and sharing. I am always amazed that with all of America's diversity and political, military and economic status in the world, many Americans are isolationists. Perhaps it's because we are such a large country and in many ways a United Nations in ourselves that we don't always think beyond our borders. The international Paralympic movement has allowed me to continue that tradition in my family of learning from other peoples and visiting other countries."

Wyeth believes that sport is a vehicle for international co-operation. Through sport human beings can express their competitive side without firing weapons, or without counting gain. They can come together in a competition that is designed to allow people to be the best that they can be and to learn from each other. Wyeth remembers, "When I competed back in 1982, there was a Dutch cyclist who had left his biking helmet back in his dormitory. It looked like he was going to be disqualified, and, without even thinking twice, I handed him my helmet so that he could compete and pursue his dream. I see that kind of co-operation over and over again, and it seems to happen more often in the world of sports than anywhere else."

Wyeth feels that this camaraderie comes from the experiences shared by many athletes with disabilities. He says, "The overwhelming majority of athletes with disabilities at some point in their lives have been told, 'You can't do that. It's not because you do not have the motivation, or the will power, or the willingness to stick to it. You cannot possibly excel in sport or in the world of work because you have a disability.' Athletes with disabilities concentrate on shifting their focus from what they can't do to what they can do."

At 32, Wyeth first competed against athletes that had similar physical characteristics, and he was thrilled by the experience. At the same time, he was realistic. He says, "Cycling has always been the love of my life, but I guess that I had the foresight to see that at age 38, as much as I enjoyed the athletic competition, we were opening doors for much younger athletes. I felt that I should move on to the equally competitive political area."

Wyeth served for 10 years on the Handicapped in Sports Committee of the United States Olympics Committee, and was on the board of the United States Cerebral Palsy Athletic Association and the steering committee for the 1984 Long Island Games. Then he decided to come out of retirement: he was selected as athlete and cycling coach for the 1988 Seoul Paralympic Games.

Although Seoul and Barcelona were heady experiences for Wyeth, the highlight for his Paralympic career was Atlanta. He says, "I don't think I ever had an experience that compared to marching into Olympic Stadium in Atlanta near the front of the US delegation and feeling the incredible rush of electricity that one feels as one is about to come out as the home team before one's home country."

Trischa Zorn:
United States

Trischa Zorn was not only the top medallist in both Barcelona and Atlanta, she is the top medallist in Paralympic history. She has earned 41 gold, 5 silver, and 3 bronze medals. No able-bodied swimmer has a record even close.

In 1992 Zorn missed making the United States Olympic team by one one-hundredth of a second. She went on to break six world records at the Barcelona Paralympics, winning ten gold and two silver medals. At the 1990 World Championships Zorn won gold in every swimming event. In Seoul in 1988 she won twelve gold medals and set nine world records.

Zorn is legally blind but began competing with non-disabled swimmers at age seven, when a coach recruited her for his relay team. She fought to win both in the pool and at school, where she sometimes had problems with a system that wasn't ready to mainstream a student with a visual disability.

Born and raised in southern California, when Zorn graduated from high school, she went on to the University of Nebraska. She was the first athlete with a physical disability to earn a full athletic scholarship in a division one school. Next she went to Indiana University and received her Master's Degree in School Administration while still training for the Barcelona Paralympics. At present she teaches children with mental disabilities in grades 1-5 at an inner-city Indianapolis school.

Zorn recalls, "Even though I had a physical disability I was treated like anybody else. If a coach wanted to deal with me differently, I would let him know I didn't want that, so everybody was very supportive."

Humour is an important part of Zorn's philosophy. She says, "I joke about myself all the time. I can laugh now at the fact that, when I first started swimming, I used to bump my head a lot on the walls. Sometimes I think that people who are not around you a lot at first are set back by humour. They are kind of like, Wow, she can joke about it. I think that it makes them more comfortable, too, because a lot of people don't know how to approach somebody with a disability."

Zorn has seen the quality of competition steadily improve since her first Paralympic event in 1980. She says, "In the early times people would swim any event — they may have swam 12 events or whatever — because the competition wasn't tough. Now it is going the way of the

Olympics. People train specifically for just one or two events, because the competition is so strong."

Although she won two gold, three silver and three bronze medals in Atlanta, Zorn is disappointed in her showing. She was recovering from surgery on both shoulders, and knew she didn't have enough time to get in the training she needed. She says, "I felt a great deal of pressure with the event being in Atlanta, but I have to look back and say I did the best that I could at the time."

Zorn was the first athlete with a disability nominated to be *Sports Illustrated*'s Athlete of the Year. She says, "It was a great honour to have people recognize your achievements as an athlete, not as somebody who has a disability, and is an athlete."

American society finds it difficult, Zorn believes, to accept those with disabilities. She says, "We knew the attendance at Atlanta was going to be bad because many of the media didn't want to stay around. They think, Who wants to see a blind person swim? Who wants to see an amputee or a dwarf run? We learn at a young age in our society that being disabled is a terrible thing. People say to their kids, Don't talk to them, or Don't stare. It is almost like disability is some kind of a disease.

"But when these people, especially the media, see the Paralympics, they are amazed, because they don't understand the elite level of competition that the Paralympics bring. We have even had doctors say, Because you can't see, you shouldn't be able to swim this fast, or jump this far. It almost exceeds the expectations of even the medical world."

Zorn struggles with the fact that Paralympic athletes in the US are not treated the same as Olympic athletes. "Other countries," she says, "have multi-sport camps where they put their Paralympic athletes in with their Olympic athletes. Our Olympic Committee needs to accept us as athletes first and realize what our potential could be."

For Zorn, disabled sport has a powerful message. "We're out to show society that just because we have a disability doesn't mean that we are limited in what we do. I want to let children or young adults who may have been involved in sports and then had an accident know that there are still things out there for them to do."

SECTION V: *Challenges For The Future*

The Paralympic movement faces some major challenges. One of these is the disparity between the developing and developed nations.

Seiichiro Ite, executive director of the Japanese Sports Association for the Disabled, says, "Recently, the view of the Paralympic Games as the Olympic Games for the disabled is getting fixed among the public. Because of this, the significance of sports for the disabled is becoming known widely. On the other hand, there is criticism that the Paralympic Games are only for the elite athletes, and the severely disabled athletes, or athletes in developing countries, are neglected."

Don Royer, former president of the ISMWSF, feels that the role of Stoke Mandeville is changing as the Paralympic Games move to the elite sport model: games at the highest level of competition. At one time, the

Stoke Mandeville Games was the ultimate goal. Royer says, "Now I see our games as more developmental in nature. When some countries cannot afford to go to world championships or to the Paralympics, or they are not at the stage where they can compete against the more established athletes in the world, it's a good transition for them to compete at Stoke for one or two years, and then get to the next stage."

Karen O'Neill, former executive director of Wheelchair Sports, and chef de mission of the Canadian team in Atlanta, says, "My hope would be a more equitable representation and depth of competitive excellence in the countries participating in the Paralympics. Right now we have probably got the top eight or nine that are starting to separate from the pack because of their resources. My hope is that we'll see more of a development approach, a sharing of resources across all countries, so it really is a full field of competitive excellence."

Akram Massarweh, vice-president of the Jordan Sports Federation for the Disabled, says,"The focus of the organisation, chaired by His

Royal Highness Prince Raid, has shifted from taking care of disabled people to involving them in competitive sport."

Sue McKiernan, secretary of the International Paralympic Committee Technical Section, sees media education as another challenge for the movement. She says, "I want to see images of the top-class athlete achieving a top class performance, not of the one that falls out of the chair or crashes. Advance preparation of the media would improve the questions they ask the athletes, the film they take of the athletes, and the photographs that are printed of the athletes."

Elizabeth Dendy, executive director of CP-ISRA, is concerned about the number of women in disabled sport. "The position of women in disabled sport really reflects what's happening to women in sport in the able-bodied world. It is up to the women themselves to make sure that they support each other, but I think that it is also important that we change the attitudes of men in positions of authority. We need changes in the culture of the institutions which, inevitably, as most of them were founded by men, are geared to men's way of doing things rather than women's.

"The statistics for women at the Paralympics in Atlanta was not a very encouraging picture. Certainly within IPC itself, and within CP-ISRA, we have women as one of our priorities, chiefly women athletes, but we are also trying to get more women in administrative positions."

Jens Bromann, IPC first vice-president, and former president of IBSA, addresses the issue of integration and its challenges. "Often when people use the word 'integration,' they use it as if to say that they would like to 'normalize' the disabled person when they integrate the disabled person into society. The way I like to see the word integration used is that both sides bend towards each other, find an understanding of each other, and then find a way to live together. Sports for the able bodied should have so great an understanding of sports for the disabled that we can find a joint concept under which we can cooperate."

Dr. Whang You Dai was the first person with a disability in Korea to become a medical doctor. Now an activist for people with a disability, she sees the Paralympic Games as a means to speed up the process of acceptance. She says, "The Seoul Paralympic Games brought many significant improvements in promoting adapted physical activities in Korea, creating more sports facilities and developing sound athletes."

Jeff Adams, wheelchair racer, sees marketing as a major challenge in disa-

bled sport, both for the benefit of individual athletes, and for the image of all those with disabilities. "Right now we have only two athletes in Canada — Chantal Petitclerc and myself — who are making quite a lot of money in sport. We haven't caught up to the able-bodied yet but we're making a good living as athletes.

"I've got professional people working for me, but we're really up against the same wall that any amateur athlete is; marketers don't like to pay money for amateur athletes. With wheelchair racing we do have an advantage in terms of being integrated with the able-bodied much more completely than a lot of

other disability groups, but it's difficult to convince people that using a disabled athlete to market is acceptable, and that people will see that as a positive message. There's such a stigma attached to it that it's difficult to break the ice.

"The whole secret to advertising is to get someone to look twice. Most advertisements people look at once, and forget. If you can make them look back, you've done your job as an advertiser. If you have an athletic commercial where you're using not only a disabled athlete who's in some cool technology — that makes people look twice — but a disabled person who is in unbelievable shape and is big and built and ripped and muscular and healthy — that makes people look three times. So you've done your job twice over as an advertiser. And they're starting slowly to catch onto that."

Ljiljana Ljubisic, athletics athlete, is concerned about the possibility of the Paralympics combining with the Olympics. "I am not for amalgamating with the Olympics. I am for using the Olympics as an educational, motivational, inspirational tool, providing opportunities for showing on a rotating calendar at the Olympics sports for the disabled: different sports, from different disabilities, rather than pushing for an acceptability of one sport, or one disability or another exclusively. I don't think that amalgamating would serve the world well, because what it is telling us is that the Paralympics are secondary games and that the Olympic ideal is still the only ideal to reach."

Ellen Stohl, activist and motivational speaker, disagrees. She says, "The Paralympics are the Olympics: the best in the world competing for gold. To keep it separate denotes the fact that we are a different group, and says that our athletic abilities aren't the same. So often people come to me and say, 'Oh, you mean the Special Olympics.' The public awareness is that 'it's only disabled people competing - isn't that nice.'

"That is not what the Paralympics is about. It's about athletes, athletes that use different means to achieve their athletic goals, but athletes nonetheless. And their quest for gold is as powerful as any other athlcte. The two games are one and the same thing: athletes competing to be the best at their sport."

In Conclusion

by Dr. Robert D. Steadward
President of the International Paralympic Committee

Ordinarily, this section would conclude our story. But this is not a conclusion; it is only a beginning. When we look at all Paralympic history as one progression, as we have been doing in this book, and when we see the unwavering upward struggle of athletes with a disability toward their goals and achievement, then we see proportionately the hopes and potential of these sport performers in the present and the future. We are in the dawn of greatness, but in the efforts and results of Winter and Summer Paralympic Games; of regional and world championships; of world records broken; of the emergence of athletes from developing nations, we behold the vision of what the 21st century can do for us and of what the human will can do with endless possibilities.

At a glance, it is nothing less than extraordinary to observe Paralympic history in the making, from 1960 when the first Paralympic Games for wheelchair athletes was organized, to 1997 and discussions with the International Olympic Committee on the inclusion of events for athletes with a disability in the Olympic Games. The years in between have produced unprecedented growth for a Movement in a comparatively embryonic stage and for the most part, present-day athletes with a disability are unlimited in their choices for sport participation.

The roots of Paralympism began with post World War II rehabilitation programs designed for veterans, many in the prime of life, with multifarious disabilities but all requiring kinesiological prescription. However, a reevaluation of the medical and psychological needs of the large number of soldiers

who were disabled in combat ultimately led to the transformation from rehabilitation to sport. In those early days more paraplegics participated in sport than other disabilities; subsequently, great strides were taken to promote and include sport for athletes with blindness, cerebral palsy, and amputations.

Undoubtedly, the most impressive growth within the Paralympic Movement has been in terms of sport excellence. Highly motivated athletes, in either the disabled or non-disabled population, experience the same ideals and the same goals, which are those of championship performance in whichever their chosen event might be. This level of sport participation is inarguably identical for every elite athlete regardless of whether or not they have a disability, or what their disability might be. It was not difficult to measure the progress: in 1968 the best time for the men's 1500m wheelchair race was 8:33.2. Today, that same event is completed in nearly 3.00 minutes. The totally blind athlete running alone down the centre lane of a 100m track covers the distance in under 11.0 seconds, incredibly close to Olympic medal times. The number of women athletes participating in both Summer and Winter Paralympic Games has significantly increased and performances steadily improved.

Perhaps the most important and recent development for

Paralympians occurred on September 22, 1989, in the City of Dusseldorf when the International Paralympic Committee was created, to act as world governing body for all athletes with a disability. I was fortunate to be elected as the inaugural President, re-elected again in 1993 and continue to hold this position. I brought to this new movement thirty years of volunteer involvement with disability sport and, most importantly, a vision - involving the use of amateur sport as a vehicle to enhance the integration of persons with a disability into all facets of community life. Primarily, my vision impressed upon the world that these opportunities are a basic right, and replaced the concept that sport opportunities for athletes with a disability were a low priority need. There has been a lack of awareness, of public interest and perhaps even a fear within all of us which reminds us how fragile life can be.

Events such as Rick Hansen's *Man In Motion* tour of wheeling 24,000 miles around the world for spinal cord injury have contributed enormously to the growing awareness of the rights, needs, and abilities of athletes with a disability. Accordingly, I believe that one of the most valuable ways to demonstrate the ability that individuals with a disability can bring to any human endeavour is through sport. My vision is based on a belief that sport for athletes with a disability can be best recognized for its true athleticism through appropriate inclusion of events with full medal status in all sporting competitions.

Hence, at the International Paralympic Committee General Assembly in Tokyo Japan, November 1995, a resolution was passed which would pave the way for discussion with the International Olympic Committee of the inclusion of two full medal status events in the 2000 Summer Paralympic Games in Sydney, Australia and beyond. The proposal has not yet gained unanimous acceptance by either the International Olympic Committee or indeed in all areas of the International Paralympic Committee. But, as it was once said, any vision involves *taking the risk of telling people what you believe, and why you believe it, and what difference it makes.*

Unquestionably, technology will make today's impossibility tomorrow's conquest; but inasmuch as this is an essential element, it will never be the determining factor. It will never stand alone, without human passion, and effort with purpose. When we consider the progress made during the past forty years, can we doubt that in the next millennium, athletes with a disability will more than realize their farthest-reaching dreams? Indeed not; they will, and we shall continue to record their moments of glory.

APPENDIX ONE

IPC Executive Committee

President	First Vice-President	Second Vice-President	Athlete's Representative	Treasurer
Dr. R.D. Steadward Canada	Dr. Jens Bromann Denmark	Dr. Nabil Salem Egypt	Mr. Manfred Kohl Germany	Mr. André Auberger France
Technical Officer	**Medical Officer**	**Member-At-Large**	**Member-At-Large**	**Member-At-Large**
Hans Lindström Sweden	Dr. Michael Riding Canada	Mr. Colin Rains England	Mrs. Marie T. Little Australia	Dr. York Y.N. Chow Hong Kong, China

Regional Representatives

Africa	America	East Asia
Mr. Harzallah Ali Tunisia	Currently Vacant	Dr. Yasuhiro Hatsuyama Japan
Europe	**Middle East**	**South Pacific**
Mr. Carl Wang Norway	Dr. Abdulhakim Al Matar Saudia Arabia	Mr. George Dunstan Australia

Sport Organization Representatives

CP-ISRA	IBSA	INAS-FMH
Miss Elizabeth Dendy United Kingdom	Mr. Enrique Sanz Jiménez Spain	Mr. Fernando Martin Vicente Spain
ISMWSF	**ISOD**	
Dr. Donald Royer Canada	Mr. Juan Palau Francas Spain	

APPENDIX TWO

Abbreviations

APOC: Atlanta Paralympics Organizing Committee
ANOC: Association of National Olympic Committees
CFSOD: Canadian Federation of Sport Organizations for the Disabled
CIAD: Commission for Inclusion of Athletes With a Disability
CIAU: Canadian Intervarsity Athletic Union Championships
CISS: Comité International de Sport des Sourds
CP-ISRA: Cerebral Palsy International Sports and Recreation Association
IBSA: International Blind Sports Association
ICC: International Coordinating Committee
INAS-FMH: International Sports Federation for Persons with Mental Handicap
IOC: International Olympic Committee
IPC: International Paralympic Committee
ISMGF: International Stoke Mandeville Games Federation
ISMWSF: International Stoke Mandeville Wheelchair Sports Federation
ISOD: International Sports Organization for the Disabled
IWF: International Wheelchair Association
LOOC: Lillehammer Olympic Organizing Committee
LPOC: Lillehammer Paralympic Organizing Committee
USFA: United States Fencing Association

APPENDIX THREE

VISTA '93

APPENDIX FOUR
Rick Hansen Centre: Edmonton, Canada

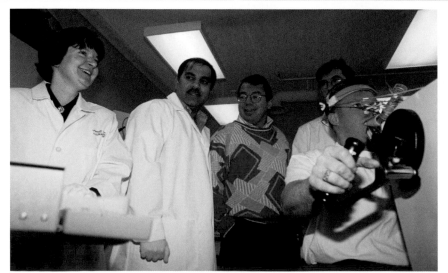

APPENDIX FIVE
Alberta Northern Lights Wheelchair Basketball Society

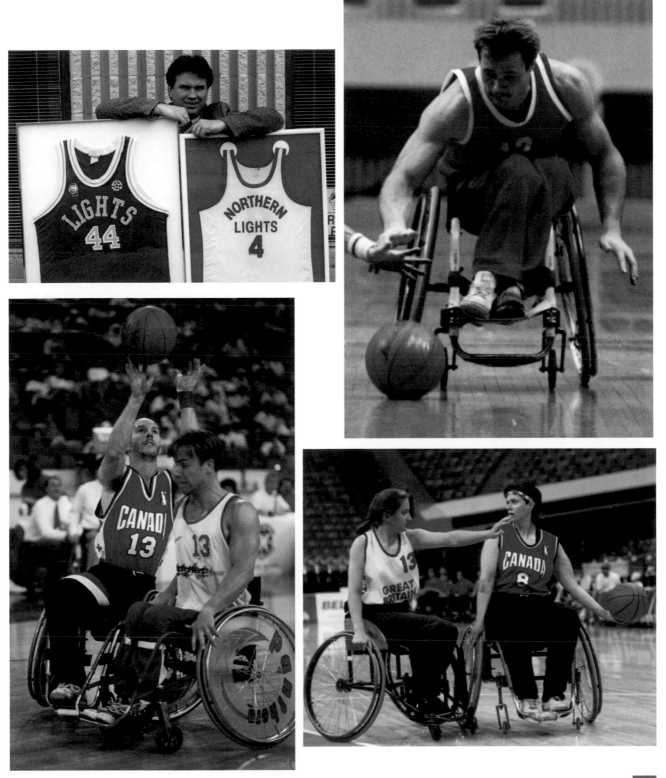

APPENDIX SIX
Acknowledgements

CANADIAN PARALYMPIC COMMITTEE

COMITÉ PARALYMPIQUE DU CANADA

Grant MacEwan Community College

Alberta Sport Recreation Parks & Wildlife Foundation

F O U N D A T I O N

An Alberta Government Lottery Funded Foundation

Audreys BOOKS LTD.

COLORFAST®

Photofinishing & Enlarging

Canon

256

We gratefully acknowledge the assistance of these individuals and companies in the production of this book.

Paul Byrne
JDI Design
David Friesen
Friesens (Book Division)
Alberta Medical Association
Lyle Best, Quikcard
Westworld Computers Education Department
Audreys Books Ltd.
Sharon & Steve Budnarchk
Creative Concepts
Gray Garner
Patrick, Courtney, and Shayne Morrison
Sarah Peterson
Jim Acton
Krishan Joshee
Doug Fulford
Leslie Shields
Pat Heydon
Dave Marvin
Ian Sterling
Paul Conrad
Marriott Management Service
Sam Mitsugi
Edmonton Journal
Patricia Shepherd
Paul De Pace
Radio Shack
Norbert, Canon

Melanie Busby
Bernie Boutin
Elmer Schaefer
Wendy Harder
Jim Dinning
Juan Antonio Samaranch
Ewen Nelson
Rick Hanson Centre
Alex Hill
Lisa Miller, CFRN TV
John Short, Edmonton Journal
Kodak
Jan Sandmark
Caterina Edwards Loverso
Jane Bishee
Shirley King
Duke' s Production (Big Del)
Telus Corporation
Roy Hermanson
Bill Dean
Justin Jeon
Angelo V. Nicosia & father
VIN
Wendy Rhodes, Rotary International

We would like to thank all those who graciously agreed to be interviewed for this book. They include:

Jeff Adams, Bernard Atha, Chantal Benoit, Matthias Berg, Jens Bromann, Barbara Campbell, Ann Cody, Chris Cohen, Mr.and Mrs. Connery, Elizabeth Dendy, Gudrun Doll-Tepper, Elaine Ell, Ron Fineran, Gray Garner, Pat Griffin, Rick Hansen, Pat Heydon, Mirre Kipfer, Thor Kleppe, Adam Lan, Hans Lindström, Ljiliana Ljubisic, Michael Massik, Reg McClellan, Peter McGregor, Sue McKiernan, Gary McPherson, Akram Massarweh, Anne Merklinger, Reinhild Möller, Barb Montemurro, Carol Mushett, Karen O'Neill, Cato Pedersen, Bob Peterson, Andre Raes, Michael Riding, Donna Ritchie, Marie Claire Ross, Don Royer, Eric Russell, Joan Scruton, Alana Shepherd, Laura Steadward, Ellen Stohl, Whang You Dai, Walter Wu, Duncan Wyeth, Pawel Zbieranowski, and Trischa Zorn.

We also wish to thank Joey Reiman, BrightHouse, for permission to use his quote:

"The Olympics is where heroes are made. The Paralympics is where heroes come."

The following have graciously granted us permission to use their photographs in this book:

American Wheelchair Basketball Association
Canadian Paralympic Committee
Canadian Wheelchair Basketball Association
Christine Chew
Lieven Coudenys
Disability Today
Laura Friar
Gray Garner
Michael Gobran
Karin Beate Nøsterud
Bob Peterson
Kazuji Shimizu
Don Weixl

Index